ENZO ANGELUCCI   PAOLO MATRICARDI

COMBAT AIRCRAFT
OF WORLD WAR II
1940-1941

Illustrations by Pierluigi Pinto

MILITARY PRESS
New York

In this poster book the tables
are designed so that if you want
you can frame them.
For the single ones cut along the dashed line,
whereas the twin tables
can be pulled out of the book
by cutting the binding thread.

This 1988 edition
published by Military Press
distributed by Crown Publishers, Inc.,
225 Park Avenue South,
New York, New York 10003
Hardcover Edition published by Orion Books

Created by ADRIANO ZANNINO
Editorial assistant SERENELLA GENOESE ZERBI
Editor: Maria Luisa Ficarra
Translated from the Italian by Ruth Taylor

Consultant for color plate Bruno Benvenuti

ISBN 0-517-64179-8

Color separation SEBI s.r.l., Milan
Typesetting Tipocrom s.r.l., Rome

Printed in Italy by SAGDOS S.p.A., Milan

THE ROLE OF THE BOMBER AT THE OUTBREAK OF WORLD WAR II

Handley Page, Caproni, Sikorsky, Ilya Mourometz, Gotha, Friedrichshafen, Zeppelin, Staaken. During World War I, these names became synonyms for heavy bombers, aircraft often enormous by the standards of the time that were capable of flying many hours before releasing their deadly bomb loads on targets. They no longer played a tactical role, such as that of the first armed biplane reconnaissance aircraft, and instead took on a decidedly strategic one. In fact, the development of the bomber and its operative use first came to maturity during the Great War. It was also during that period that the foundations for the further development of this type of aircraft were laid, although despite the great technological progress that took place during the 1920s and 1930s in the field of engines, airframes, and materials, the true potential of the bomber had still been only partially exploited on the eve of the new conflict. Its strategic role was particularly underestimated, despite the fact that twenty years earlier, with the beginning of massive air raids concentrated on a single target, it had played a determining part in the final stages of the conflict. The reasons for this were many and varied from country to country, linked not only to differences in industrial potential, but above all to differences in military theories and differences in the rates of the rearmament programs that had been launched, especially in the European nations, during the 1930s. In fact, on September 1, 1939, the date of the outbreak of World War II, not one of the belligerent nations had a modern four-engine heavy bomber in service. The standard aircraft was a two-engine medium bomber, which was fast but had a rather modest range and bomb load and continued to operate in a fundamentally tactical role, despite being sometimes classified as strategic. In the period between the two wars, the two-engine formula eventually established itself in all the more aeronautically advanced nations, with the single exception of Italy, where there was a particularly strong tradition of design and construction based on the use of three engines in larger type aircraft. But what was the situation as far as the principal air forces involved in the conflict were concerned and what were their prospects on the eve of the war's outbreak? Let us examine them briefly.

In Germany, the Luftwaffe continued to hide behind the activities of commercial aviation even after it had been founded officially. Junkers, Heinkel, and Dornier, Germany's three great manufacturers of bombers, gained great experience from this ambiguous situation, and many of the aircraft that were subsequently to become symbols of the war made their debut bearing civilian insignia. Right from the start, production was concentrated on two-engine and single-engine models; the only exception, in later years, was the four-engine Heinkel He.177. This was the only strategic bomber to go into service in the Luftwaffe, but for many complex reasons, its use did not represent a change in thinking: the German air force remained dedicated to primarily tactical theories, tested so successfully in the course of the Spanish Civil War. When World War II broke out, the Luftwaffe's principal bombers were the two-engine Dornier Do.17, Junkers Ju.88, and Heinkel He.111 and the single-engine Junkers Ju.87. These aircraft were never replaced by new and more effective models, although they underwent constant development in the course of the conflict. The same could not be said of Great Britain, although in 1939 the RAF's bomber force still consisted of aircraft designed at the beginning of the decade. The principal types in service were the single-engine Vickers Wellesley and Fairey Battle and the two-engine Armstrong Whitworth Whitley, Bristol Blenheim, Handley Page Hampden, and Vickers Wellington. These aircraft bore the entire brunt of the initial phase of the war, but a recovery was not long in coming. Since 1936 the General Staff had launched a program for the construction of four-engine heavy bombers. The new aircraft included the Short Stirling, the Handley Page Halifax, and the Avro Lancaster. Although the war had reached an advanced stage when they went into operation, they played a determining role in the conflict in Europe.

In Italy, too, the *Regia Aeronautica* prepared for the conflict on the basis of combat experiences during the Spanish Civil War that had given a false impression of the effective potential of its aircraft. However, unlike its ally the Luftwaffe, neither the quality or quantity of its bombers had undergone any visible improvements. When the war broke out, the principal types in service were the two-engine Fiat B.R.20 and the three-engine Savoia Marchetti SM.79 and CANT Z.1007 *bis*. Although they could be considered generally effective in an international confrontation, they actually lacked adequate defense and were very vulnerable. Nevertheless, these aircraft were to remain virtually unaltered for the entire duration of the war, and they continued to represent the standard of the front line. In particular, Italy undertook the construction of a true strategic bomber (the excellent Piaggio P.108) very late.

France's sudden disappearance from the scene of the conflict eliminated any means of recording a significant development in its bombers. However, on the eve of the war, the outdated planning of the *Armée de l'Air* became clear. When the war broke out, obsolete bombers such as the Amiot 143 and the Bloch 200 and 210 were still in service, and the plans for a restrengthening, subsequently interrupted by the German occupation, had not included the introduction of strategic bombers: the bombers in preparation were light or medium two-engine aircraft, destined for use in a fundamentally tactical role, such as the Potez 630, LeO 451, Amiot 351, and 354. The planning of the Soviet air force also remained primarily tactical, despite a long tradition in the construction of large multiengine bombers: in 1939, the Tupolev TB-3s still in service had been surpassed in their front-line duties, while the more modern four-engine Petlyakov Pe-8 strategic bomber never really proved up to the situation. Following the two-engine Tupolev SB-2s, which had caused so much astonishment in Spain, thanks to their excellent performance, the structure of the VVS (Voenno Vosnusniye Sili) continued to be based on other light and medium bombers, such

as the Ilyushin Il-4, the Tupolev Tu-2, and the Petlyakov Pe-2.

The United States and Japan deserve to be discussed separately. While the war raged in Europe, on the other side of the world the other two protagonists were still preparing their air forces. However, in Japan the bomber force followed a development similar to that in Germany, with the main types still remaining two-engine medium bombers, both in the army air force and the navy air force. However, in the United States, the years immediately prior to the war were used to bridge the existing gap and to start work on an entirely new generation of bombers, the development of which definitively influenced the course of the war and eventually became influential throughout the world. This development did not concern only the category of light and medium bombers (including the excellent two-engine Douglas, North American, and Martin) but also and above all that of the great four-engine heavy bombers. The first of these was the immortal Boeing B-17, and the second the Consolidated B-24 Liberator. Their fame was second only to that of the last strategic bomber of the war: the Boeing B-29.

1941

February 6	The British occupy Benghazi. On February 9 bombard Pisa and Leghorn.
March 1	Bulgaria adheres to the Tripartite Pact.
March 27-28	Together with Rommel's expedition corps, Italian troops begin a new offensive in Cyrenaica.
April 5	Signing of a friendship pact between the Soviet Union and Yugoslavia.
April 6	Hitler invades Yugoslavia and declares war on Greece. On April 17, Yugoslavia surrenders.
May 27	The German battleship *Bismarck* is sunk in the Atlantic by British aeronaval forces.
June 22	Hitler launches the invasion of the Soviet Union (Operation Barbarossa). Germany's allies are Italy, Rumania, Hungary, and Finland.
July 12	Pact signed between the Soviet Union and Great Britain for common action against Germany.
August 14	Churchill and Roosevelt sign the Atlantic Charter.
October 16	General Hideki Tojo, leader of the extremists, becomes head of government in Tokyo following the resignation of the moderate Prince Konoye.
November 7	400 RAF bombers carry out a massive air raid on Berlin.
December 7	The Japanese attack the American naval base of Pearl Harbor without warning, using 423 aircraft that took off from six aircraft carriers. Five battleships and two cruisers are sunk, while the majority of the American aircraft based in Hawaii are destroyed.
December 8	The United States and Great Britain declare war on Japan.
December 10	The Japanese invade the Philippines and sink the British battleships *Prince of Wales* and *Repulse* off the Malaysian coast.
December 11	Italy and Germany declare war on the United States.
December 17	The Italians and Germans withdraw from Libya.
December 25	The Japanese force Hong Kong to surrender.

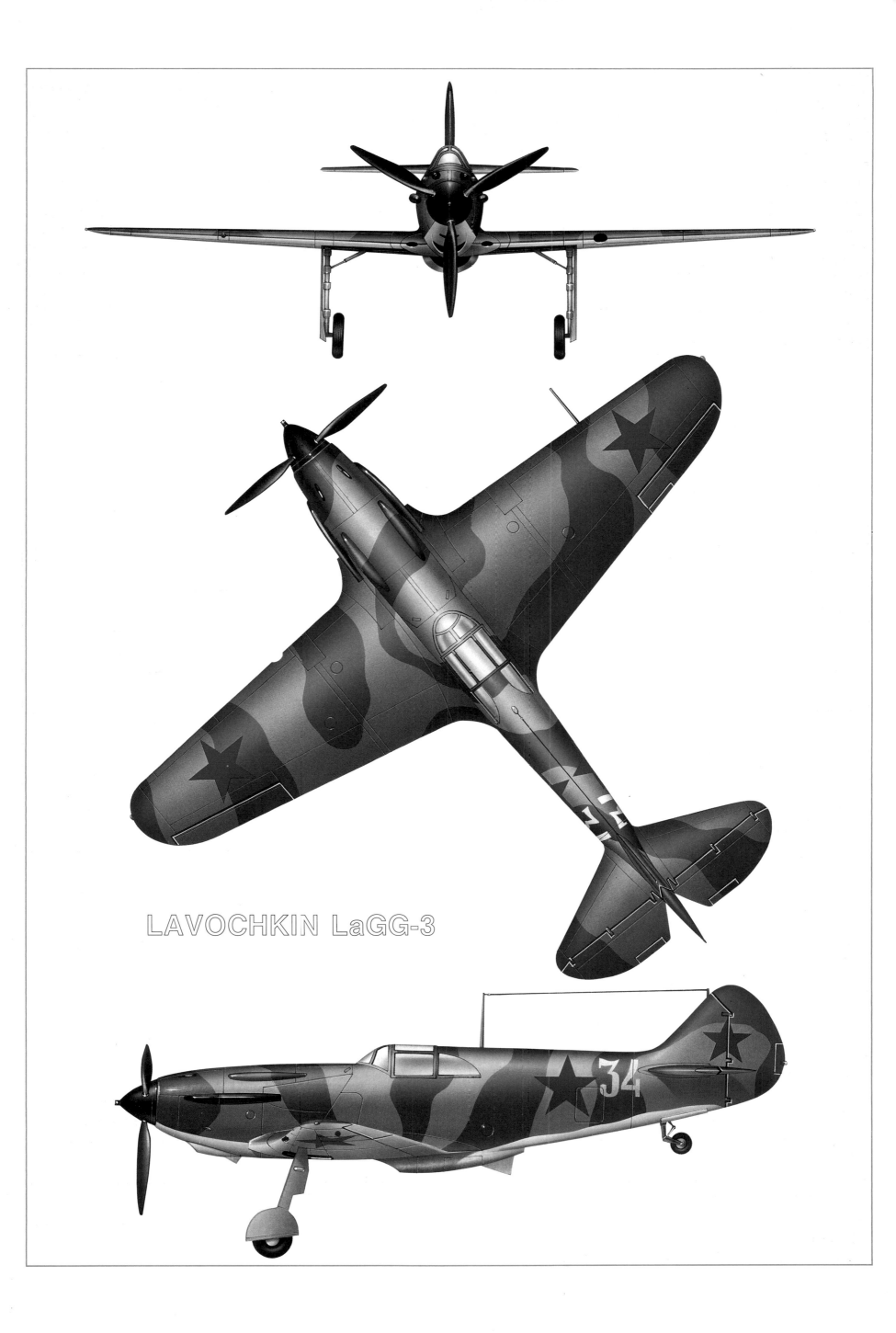

LAVOCHKIN LaGG-3

The generation of combat aircraft built in the Soviet Union during the war witnessed the debut of designers who were to become world famous over the next few years. Following Mikoyan and Gurevich, another extremely talented technician was Semyon Alexseyevich Lavochkin, whose initials characterized a family of fighters that survived until the 1950s, ranging from the LaGG-1 of 1940, to the La-11 of 1947, the last aircraft powered by a piston engine to serve in the Soviet air force.

Lavochkin executed his first project together with another two talented technicians, Vladimir Petrovich Gorbunov and Mikhail Ivanovich Gudkov, with whom he had worked since 1938. This was a single-seater fighter, initially designated I-22 and then LaGG-1; the prototype made its maiden flight on March 30, 1940. The aircraft was a low-wing monoplane, carefully studied from an aerodynamic point of view and fitted with completely retractable landing gear. A predominant feature that made it unique among its kind, was its being built entirely in wood, with the exception of the moving parts, which were metal, and the fabric covering: the fuselage, empennage, and wings had a supporting structure in wood onto which a covering of diagonal strips of plywood was stuck using special resins. Its engine was a large Klimov M-105 liquid-cooled V-12 that generated 1,050 hp at takeoff.

However, flight tests proved to be unsatisfactory. Consequently, before production got under way, numerous modifications were carried out. These included the adoption of a more powerful and supercharged version of the M-105 engine and of a three-bladed variable-pitch metal propeller, increased fuel tank capacity, and the installation of slats on the leading edge of the wings. The prototype was redesignated I-301 and, once tests had been com-

A snow-covered Soviet Air Force LaGG-3.

color plate
Lavochkin LaGG-3 Soviet Air Force - USSR 1942

Aircraft:	Lavochkin LaGG-3
Nation:	USSR
Manufacturer:	State Industries
Type:	Fighter
Year:	1941
Engine:	Klimov M-105 P, 12-cylinder V, liquid-cooled, 1,050 hp
Wingspan:	32 ft 2 in (9.80 m)
Length:	29 ft 1 in (8.86 m)
Height:	8 ft 10 in (2.69 m)
Weight:	7,032 lb (3,190 kg)
Maximum speed:	348 mph (560 km/h) at 16,400 ft (5,000 m)
Ceiling:	31,500 ft (9,690 m)
Range:	404 miles (650 km)
Armament:	1 × 20 mm cannon; 2 machine guns; 440 lb (200 kg) of bombs
Crew:	1

Above, a captured LaGG-3 employed by the Finnish Air Force; below, German ground crewmen repair a captured LaGG-3.

pleted, the fighter went into production with the official designation LaGG-3. However, its initial operative service (from 1941) brought to light some negative flight characteristics, for example, a tendency to go into a spin following particularly tight turns, making further research and testing necessary.

Once in service with the units, the LaGG-3 was widely used in the early phases of the war against the Germans, especially on the Finnish front, and its performance proved to be satisfactory. However, the aircraft never possessed the characteristics of an interceptor that had been planned in the original project. Nevertheless, it was used with success in bomber escort duty, ground attack, and target attack against the least dangerous of the formidable German fighters, such as reconnaissance planes and bombers. Moreover, the LaGG-3 proved to be extremely versatile and reliable. Its typical armament included a 20 mm cannon that fired through the propeller hub and two 12.7 mm machine guns, while under the wings supports were planned for light bombs or rockets. Up to August 1942, a total of 6,528 LaGG-3s came off the assembly lines, a remarkable number considering the unexceptional performance of the aircraft.

In the course of production numerous other experimental prototypes were completed, built with the aim of improving the aircraft's characteristics. Lavochkin, in particular, dedicated himself to the task of perfecting it. Following a series of failed attempts, success was achieved when a radically new engine became available. This was the Shvetsov M.82 radial engine and, once it had been fitted on the LaGG-3, it transformed it into a first-class aircraft: the LaGG-5 of 1942, one of the best Soviet fighters of the entire war.

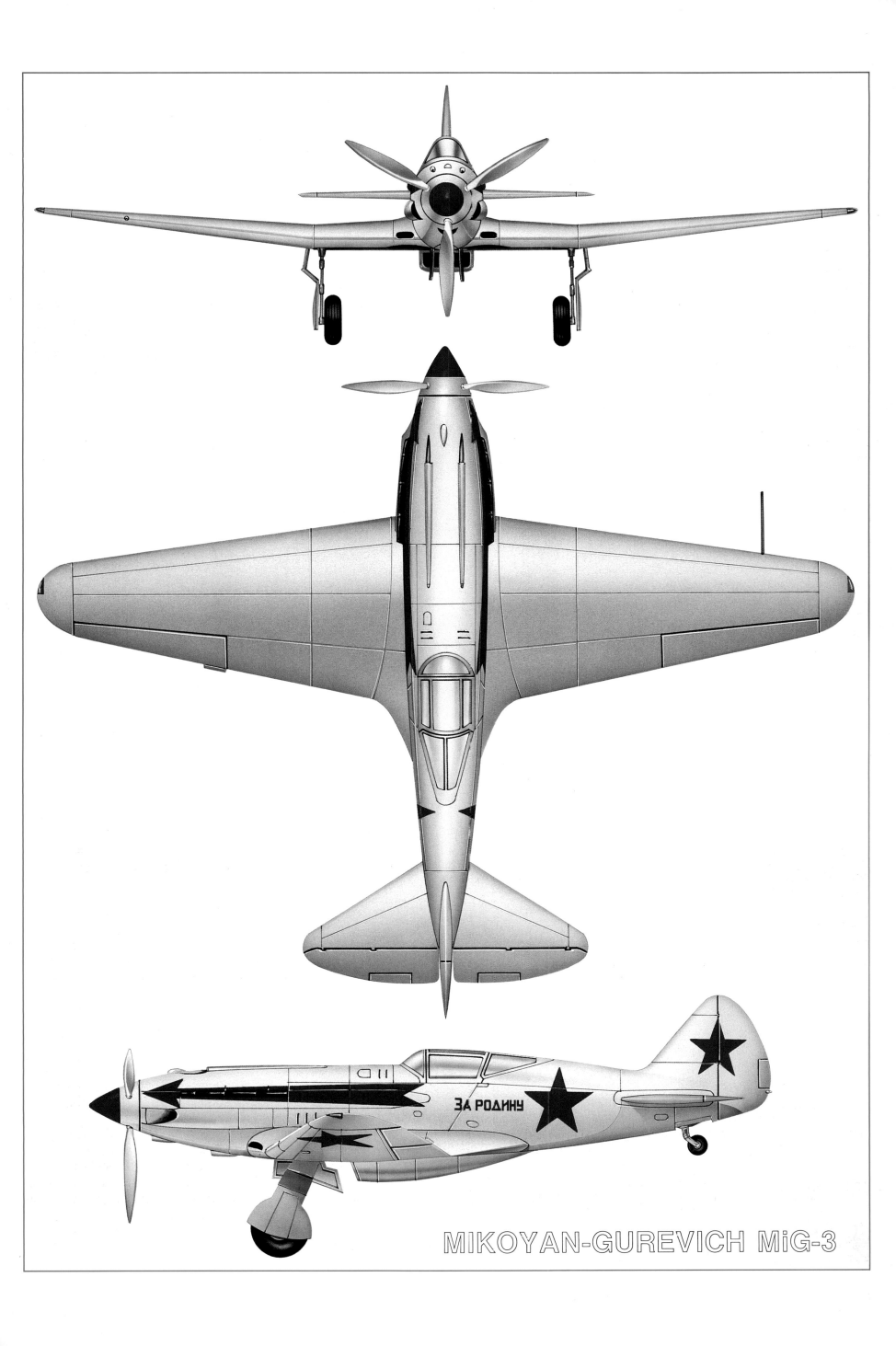

MIKOYAN-GUREVICH MiG-3

The MiG-1 was the first Soviet fighter of World War II and the first to bear the "signature" of Artem Ivanovich Mikoyan and Mikhail Iossipovich Gurevich, two designers who were to become world famous. Even today, despite the death of Mikoyan in 1970, and that of Gurevich in 1976, the designation MiG continues to be used to identify the most advanced Soviet combat aircraft, in remembrance of the partnership between the two great technicians, which originated in 1938, immediately prior to the outbreak of war.

In that year, Mikoyan and Gurevich began their long association with the intention of building a single-seater interceptor developed around the large and powerful Mikulin AM-35, a 12-cylinder V engine capable of generating 1,200 hp at 19,735 ft (6,000 m) and 1,350 hp at takeoff. Two projects were completed, although only work on the second went ahead: designated MiG-1, it was a small, slim low-wing monoplane, with retractable landing gear. Its airframe and covering were composite, wood and metal. In practice, it was the smallest and most compact airframe that could be created around the heavy engine, one of the most powerful in its category in the world at the time.

The prototype, redesignated I-200, was completed in only four months, and it made its maiden flight on April 5, 1940. During initial flight testing the aircraft proved to have an excellent performance as far as speed was concerned, touching 403 mph (648.5 km/h) at 22,640 ft (6,900 m) on May 24. Mass production was launched immediately, although the fighter was not without faults. The principal ones were its lack of maneuverability, its negative characteristics in flight (due to the excessive weight of the wings), its limited range, and a lack of protection and armament.

These problems caused production to be limited to 100 aircraft and led the designers to develop a new version. This was designated MiG-3 and began to reach the units at the beginning of 1941, proving to be greatly superior to the previous aircraft. In particular, its overall aerodynamic characteristics had been improved; larger fuel tanks were installed; in the cockpit the pilot's seat and the canopy were modified; the engine was rendered more powerful, due also to the installation of a new propeller.

In combat the MiG-3 displayed its potential to the full, proving capable of giving the best of its performance at altitudes over 16,450 ft (5,000 m), where it was able to compete on equal terms with the best adversaries. However, at lower altitudes there was a noticeable decrease in the fighter's overall performance and in its maneuverability that placed it in inferior conditions. The aircraft's armament constituted another weak point: the two 7.62 mm machine guns and the single 12.7 mm machine gun and the 440 lb (200 kg) of bombs were clearly not enough; various experiments were attempted to remedy this, but the use of heavier weapons seriously penalized the aircraft's qualities.

However, the MiG-3 always remained a transitional aircraft, while the Soviets were awaiting more modern and effective products (like the Yakovlev and Lavochkin fighters) with which they finally succeeded in gaining overall superiority compared to the Luftwaffe. Production of the MiG-3 was suspended in the spring of 1942, when building of the AM-35A engine ceased after it had made way for the more powerful AM-38, destined for the Ilyushin Il-2. A total of 3,322 were built, in addition to the 100 MiG-1s. However, Mikoyan and Gurevich's fighter remained in front-line service until the final months of 1943, and it was subsequently relegated to secondary roles.

---

color plate
MiG-3 34th IAP (Moscow Hawks) Soviet Air Force - Moscow-Vnukovo 1941

Aircraft:	Mikoyan-Gurevich MiG-3
Nation:	USSR
Manufacturer:	State Industries
Type:	Fighter
Year:	1941
Engine:	Mikulin AM-35A, 12-cylinder V, liquid-cooled, 1,350 hp
Wingspan:	33 ft 9 1/2 in (10.28 m)
Length:	26 ft 9 in (8.15 m)
Height:	11 ft 6 in (3.54 m)
Weight:	7,385 lb (3,356 kg) loaded
Maximum speed:	407 mph (655 km/h) at 22,960 ft (7,000 m)
Ceiling:	39,370 ft (12,000 m)
Range:	510 miles (820 km)
Armament:	3 machine guns; 440 lb (200 kg) of bombs
Crew:	1

MiG-3 in winter camouflage with red wings.

SUKHOI Su-2

Pavel Osipovich Sukhoi, still famous today for some of the most modern combat aircraft in service in the Soviet air force, began his career as a designer in 1924, as part of a team headed by Tupolev. Twelve years later, in 1936, he set to work on the study of a low-wing single-engine bomber-reconnaissance plane with retractable landing gear. This aircraft was designated ANT-51, and its prototype took to the air on August 25, 1937, but it did not prove reliable enough to go into production. Sukhoi stuck to his chosen formula and a year later, when he was made responsible for an independent team, he continued to develop the project and built a series of prototypes from which the Su-2 model of 1940 derived. This was an attack aircraft, and although it was clearly transitional it bore the brunt of much of the fighting during the early phases of the war until the reorganization of the Soviet aeronautical industry led to the creation of its more illustrious successor, the Ilyushin Il-2.

The Sukhoi Su-2 (originally designated BB-1, the letters indicating the role of medium-range bomber) was an all-metal low-wing monoplane of remarkable size, with retractable landing gear and a two-man crew housed in a long, completely glazed cockpit that had a turret to its rear. Originally the aircraft was powered by a 950 hp Shvetsov M-88 radial engine, while its defensive armament consisted of four 7.62 mm ShKas machine guns installed in the wings and a fifth machine gun mounted in the turret on the back for the observer-bombardier. The weight of the bomb load reached 1,325 lb (600 kg) and, if necessary, it could be carried entirely inside the fuselage.

In service from 1940, the Sukhoi nevertheless proved to have a series of faults and limitations, many of which were similar to those of aircraft in the same category produced by other nations. These included a lack of maneuverability, a rather disappointing overall performance, and inadequate defensive armament. Consequently, efforts were made to improve the aircraft during the entire period of production, which according to reliable estimates, exceeded 2,000 planes. The engine, in particular, was subject to the most radical changes: a 1,000 hp M-88B engine was used initially, then, in the final series, the choice fell on the more powerful 1,400 hp M-82. On the one hand, the increase in power improved the aircraft's performance, especially its maximum speed, but on the other, its overall flying characteristics were penalized.

Further modifications were carried out on the armament: some aircraft were provided with a second machine gun in the turret, while others had a weapon installed in a retractable housing in the belly. However, in the end, a compromise was reached by reducing the machine guns on the wings to two, and the bomb load to 880 lb (400 kg).

Even after the appearance of the more effective Ilyushin Il-2, Sukhoi proceeded with the development of his aircraft. At the end of 1941 he built a variant (designated Su-4) in which he installed the experimental Shvetsov M-90 engine generating no fewer than 2,100 hp. The aircraft was tested in December 1941, but it never went into production. A similar fate awaited the more effective and powerful Su-6 which was never produced in any great number, despite being superior in some ways to its Ilyushin rival. The fate of this aircraft, whose development had begun in 1939, was influenced by the length of time needed to tune the engine (a 2,000 hp Shvetsov M-71 18-cylinder radial); the developmental phase continued, amidst great difficulties, until December 1940. The development of the project proceeded with the Su-6-II model of 1942, built with the idea of developing it simoultaneously with the Ilyushin Il-2, and the Su-6-III, powered by a 2,000 hp AM-42 liquid-cooled engine, which began flight testing early in 1944.

Once again, neither of these two aircraft reached the mass production stage.

---

color plate

Sukhoi Su-2 Soviet Air Force - USSR 1942

Aircraft:	Sukhoi Su-2
Nation:	USSR
Manufacturer:	State Industries
Type:	Bomber
Year:	1940
Engine:	Shvetsov M-82, 14-cylinder radial, air-cooled, 1,400 hp
Wingspan:	46 ft 11 in (14.30 m)
Length:	34 ft 4 in (10.46 m)
Height:	12 ft 3 in (3.75 m)
Takeoff weight:	10,362 lb (4,700 kg) loaded
Maximum speed:	302 mph (485 km/h) at 19,190 ft (5,850 m)
Ceiling:	29,605 ft (9,000 m)
Range:	683 miles (1,100 km)
Armament:	5 machine guns; 1,325 lb (600 kg) of bombs
Crew:	2

An early model of the Sukhoi Su-2.

THE SOVIET UNION

As in the case of the United States, in the Soviet Union the phase of decisive strengthening of the air force took place once it had become directly involved in the conflict. The great progress achieved during the 1930s (and above all the effectiveness of several aircraft, including the Polikarpov I-16 fighters and the Tupolev SB-2 bombers, which had proved to be clearly superior to the aircraft of the major European nations during the Spanish Civil War) had led to the Soviet Union acquiring a false impression of its air force's effective potential. When the German invasion took place in June 1941, what had been considered one of the most powerful air forces in the world was literally overwhelmed by the overall superiority of the Luftwaffe, and the quantity of aircraft at the disposal of the Soviet Union proved incapable of withstanding the quality of those of the enemy. At the time, the units of the VVS (Voenno Vosnusniye Sili) were still being completely reorganized and were paradoxically equipped with the same aircraft as in the previous decade, the new models destined to replace them were not yet operative, either because they were still at an experimental stage or because production had not yet got under way. According to an official Soviet report, in the first nine hours of Operation Barbarossa (June 22, 1941) the Germans destroyed 1,200 aircraft, 800 of which were on the ground, and they gained supremacy in the air. At a strictly operational level, the weeks that followed consolidated this ratio of strength.

However, the reaction was not long in coming, even though more than a year was to pass before the balance weighed in favor of the Soviets. The effort at recovery was enormous and was helped by the arrival of winter, which reduced the intensity and effectiveness of the German air operations on the one hand, while on the other it made it possible for the Soviet Union to put into action one of the most important strategic decisions made during 1941: the removal of the war industry to sites far from the front, discussed for the first time in the Kremlin on August 19. In those circumstances, it was the only possible step toward a reorganization of the industrial network that would make it competitive once more. During the winter months, more than 600 factories were transferred to areas that were considered safe: the region of the Volga, the Urals, and western Siberia. Whole aircraft and engine factories were dismantled and rebuilt, often in emergency conditions, and study and research centers were transferred with them.

This long and complex process caused many problems. The most significant one was a great slowing down in aeronautical production, which despite having reached a total of 15,735 aircraft of all types in 1941, literally collapsed in the second half of the year and during the early months of 1942: 1,039 aircraft completed in January, 915 in February, and 1,647 in March. However, in the end, the results compensated for the immense effort. In fact, the initial recovery took place in 1942. This was not only from a quantitative point of view but also from a qualitative one, with the appearance of aircraft, the results of new projects, that contributed to reestablishing the balance of power with the Luftwaffe, especially as far as fighters and attack aircraft were concerned.

Chronology

1940

January 13. The prototype of the Yakovlev Ya-26, from which the Yak-1 fighter was to be derived, takes to the air. This aircraft (of which 8,721 were built) became the progenitor of a large family of combat planes, totaling approximately 30,000 aircraft in all.

April 5. The I-200 prototype takes to the air. The MiG-1, the first aircraft to bear the initials of the famous designers Mikoyan and Gurevich, was to be developed from it.

October 12. The Ilyushin TsKB-57 takes to the air. The Il-2 Sturmovik, the Soviet Union's most famous attack aircraft of the war, was derived from this definitive prototype, a total of more than 35,000 being built in various versions.

1941

January 28. The Tupolev ANT-58 makes its maiden flight. The Tu-2 was to be developed from this prototype and was to become the Soviet Union's second medium bomber, from the point of view of importance and quantity, during the conflict. It remained in production from 1942 until 1948, and in service until the 1950s.

June 22. Hitler launches Operation Barbarossa, a massive attack against the Soviet Union that extended from the Baltic to the Black Sea.

June 23. The Soviet airline (Aeroflot) is mobilized to combat the German invasion: aircraft and personnel were placed at the armed forces' disposal for transport duties. From October to December, the action around Leningrad was particularly intense.

August 7/8. Il-4 bombers belonging to the Soviet naval aviation carry out a raid on Berlin. The mission was a reprisal following the heavy bombing attacks carried out by the Luftwaffe on Moscow, the first of which took place on the night of July 21/22.

August 27. First contact between Soviet aircraft and those of the Italian Expedition Corps (CSIR) in the Soviet Union. The command of this unit had been organized on July 30 to back the German invasion.

PETLYAKOV Pe-8

PETLYAKOV Pe-8

The Petlyakov Pe-8 used by Soviet foreign minister Molotov photographed during a refueling stop in Scotland while on a flight to Washington in May 1942.

The Petlyakov Pe-8 was the only four-engine bomber put into service by the Soviet Union during World War II. Nevertheless, this large aircraft was never a particularly effective combat plane, and throughout the entire period of its production it was plagued by difficulties in engine-tuning. From 1939 until October 1941, only 79 aircraft came off the assembly lines: the Pe-8 went into service in May 1940 and remained there for almost the entire duration of the war, although it was gradually relegated to secondary roles. Apart from the numerous raids carried out on German territory, and on Berlin in particular, the Petlyakov bomber should be remembered especially for some of the remarkably long flights that it made, both during the war and after. These included a journey from Moscow to Washington and back on a diplomatic mission, with stops in Scotland, Iceland, and Canada on a flight totaling some 11,000 miles (17,700 km) that took place between May 19 and June 13, 1942.

The project was launched in 1934 by a team headed by Andrei Nicolaevich Tupolev that also included Vladimir Mikhailovich Petlyakov, in response to precise specifications requesting a modern four-engine strategic bomber, capable of reaching its maximum speed at an altitude of 26,315 ft (8,000 m). Originally designated ANT-42, the prototype took to the air for the first time on December 27, 1936. The solution chosen to guarantee supercharging to the four 1,100 hp Mikulin M-100 engines was unusual: by means of a supercharger installed in the fuselage that also drove a fifth M-100 engine. This arrangement was tested in 1937 and improved in the second prototype, which took to the air on July 26 the following year. This solution proved capable of guaranteeing the requested performance at high altitudes: the bomber's maximum speed was superior even to that of the German Messerschmitt Bf.109B and Heinkel He.112 fighters. The Pe-8 (it assumed this designation in 1941) was an all-metal aircraft, provided with a crew of 11 men and defensive armament consisting of four machine guns and two 20 mm cannons installed in turrets and in two positions in the rear part of the internal engine nacelles. As for its bomb load, it could carry a maximum of 8,830 lb (4,000 kg).

In 1939, the building of five preseries aircraft was authorized definitively and, in these aircraft, a radical change in the power plants (supercharged Mikulin AM-35As, generating 1,350 hp each)

rendered the complicated "centralized" supercharge system totally unnecessary. Deliveries to the units commenced in May 1940, but on the whole the aircraft's performance was disappointing. Thus a long search for more efficient engines began: first four ACh-30B diesel engines generating 1,500 hp each were installed, but they did not prove to be very reliable; then after production of the AM-35A engines ceased, M-82 and M-82FN Shvetsov radial engines were chosen (the latter were capable of generating no fewer than 1,700 hp), and they were fitted onto approximately fifty production series aircraft.

The final series also incorporated several aerodynamic improvements, devised by Iosif Formich Nyezval, who had succeeded Petlyakov, following his death in an aircraft accident in 1942. However, the Pe-8 never achieved an optimum configuration, due to a lack of interest on the part of the Soviet military authorities, who were more than satisfied with the performance of the two-engine Ilyushin Il-4. Nevertheless, approximately 30 Pe-8s survived the war and remained in service until the late 1950s.

---

color plate
Petlyakov Pe-8 Soviet Air Force - USSR. Personal aircraft of the foreign minister Molotov

---

Aircraft:	Petlyakov Pe-8
Nation:	USSR
Manufacturer:	State Industries
Type:	Bomber
Year:	1940
Engine:	4 Mikulin AM-35A, 12-cylinder V, liquid-cooled, 1,350 hp each
Wingspan:	128 ft 3 1/3 in (39.10 m)
Length:	77 ft 4 3/4 in (23.59 m)
Height:	20 ft 4 in (6.20 m)
Takeoff weight:	69,268 lb (31,420 kg)
Maximum speed:	265 mph (427 km/h) at 20,920 ft (6,360 m)
Ceiling:	27,560 ft (8,400 m)
Range:	2,920 miles (4,700 km)
Armament:	2 × 20 mm cannons; 4 machine guns; 8,830 lb (4,000 kg) of bombs
Crew:	11

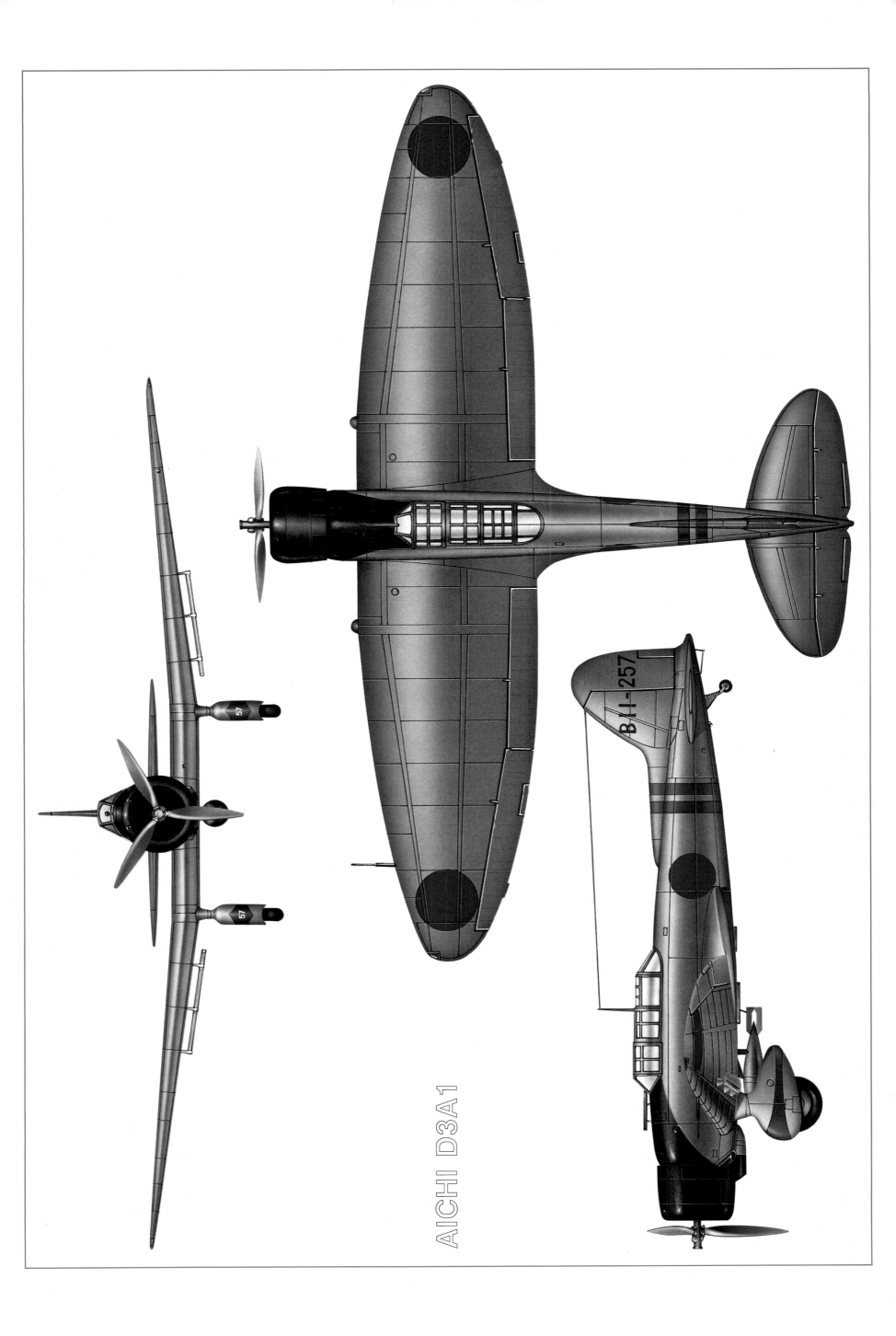

AICHI D3A1

AICHI D3A

The last carrier-based Japanese aircraft to have fixed landing gear, the Aichi D3A was also the first aircraft bearing the insignia of the Rising Sun to bomb American targets. This occurred on the morning of December 7, 1941, at Pearl Harbor, when 126 VALs (as the aircraft was known in the Allies' identification code) comprised the bulk of the Japanese bomber formations. Despite its apparently outdated lines and its rather modest overall performance, this large single-engine aircraft eventually proved to be one of the best dive-bombers of its time and was extremely successful in the Pacific during the first year of the war. In the course of its long and extensive operational career, the Aichi D3A was the aircraft that succeeded in sinking the greatest number of Allied warships, including the British aircraft carrier H.M.S. *Hermes* and the cruisers *Cornwall* and *Dorsetshire* in April 1942. In the course of these missions, the Japanese pilots succeeded in dropping more than 80 percent of their bomb loads on target.

The D3A originated in the summer of 1936, when the Imperial Navy invited bids for the manufacture of a dive-bomber to replace the old D1A2 biplanes. Aichi, Nakajima, and Mitsubishi all responded with proposals, although only the first two companies remained in the competition. The Aichi prototype made its maiden flight in January 1938. It was an all-metal low-wing monoplane with fixed and faired main landing gear powered by a 710 hp Nakajima Hikari radial engine. The wing plan was elliptical and was similar to that of the German Heinkel He.70. The aircraft was also provided with aerodynamic brakes similar to those fitted on the Junkers Ju.87 Stuka. It had a traditional empennage and a circular section fuselage. The two crew members were housed in a long, completely glazed cockpit.

A series of problems emerged during the first flight tests: in particular, the aircraft was underpowered and proved to be unstable when carrying out tight turns, while the aerodynamic brakes were inadequate. Consequently, a second prototype had to be built with modifications to the wing and diving brakes, as well as a more powerful engine (an 840 hp Mitsubishi Kinsei 3). With these improvements, the Aichi D3A proved to be generally superior to its Nakajima rival and, in December 1939, it was chosen to go into production. This commenced at the beginning of the following year and continued for almost the entire duration of the conflict: up to August 1945, a total of 1,495 aircraft were completed in two principal versions.

Testing of the initial D3A1 variant (powered by a 1,000 hp Kinsei 43 engine) took place on board the aircraft carriers *Kaga* and *Akagi*, and during 1940 the aircraft was assigned to the remaining units of the Imperial Navy. The second version, the D3A2, replaced the first in the autumn of 1942, the principal modifications consisting of the fitting of a 1,300 hp Kinsei 54 engine and of much larger fuel tanks. A total of approximately 1,000 of these aircraft were completed, and the Showa Hikoki Kogyo was also called upon to build them, producing 201 aircraft between December 1942 and August 1945. However, with the appearance of the faster Yokosuka D4Y Suisei, the Aichi D3A was gradually relegated to the less important aircraft carriers and to land-based units and, from 1944, the surviving aircraft began to equip training units. As in the case of many Japanese aircraft, its final destination was that of the suicide missions, although in this desperate role the D3As proved to be particularly vulnerable when faced with the powerful and experienced American fighters: in fact, losses were very heavy, without producing particularly remarkable results.

color plate
Aichi D3A1 *Hiryu* aircraft carrier Imperial Japanese Navy Air Force
Pearl Harbor strike - December 1941

Aircraft:	Aichi D3A1
Nation:	Japan
Manufacturer:	Aichi Kokuki KK
Type:	Bomber
Year:	1940
Engine:	Mitsubishi Kinsei 43, 14-cylinder radial, air-cooled, 1,000 hp
Wingspan:	47 ft 2 in (14.38 in)
Length:	33 ft 5 1/2 in (10.19 m)
Height:	12 ft 7 1/2 in (3.84 m)
Weight:	8,047 lb (3,650 kg) loaded
Maximum speed:	240 mph (386 km/h) at 9,840 ft (3,000 m)
Ceiling:	30,050 ft (9,300 m)
Range:	915 miles (1,472 km)
Armament:	3 machine guns; 813 lb (370 kg) of bombs
Crew:	2

A formation of Aichi D3As during a training flight. The aircraft belong to a training unit for carrier-based planes.

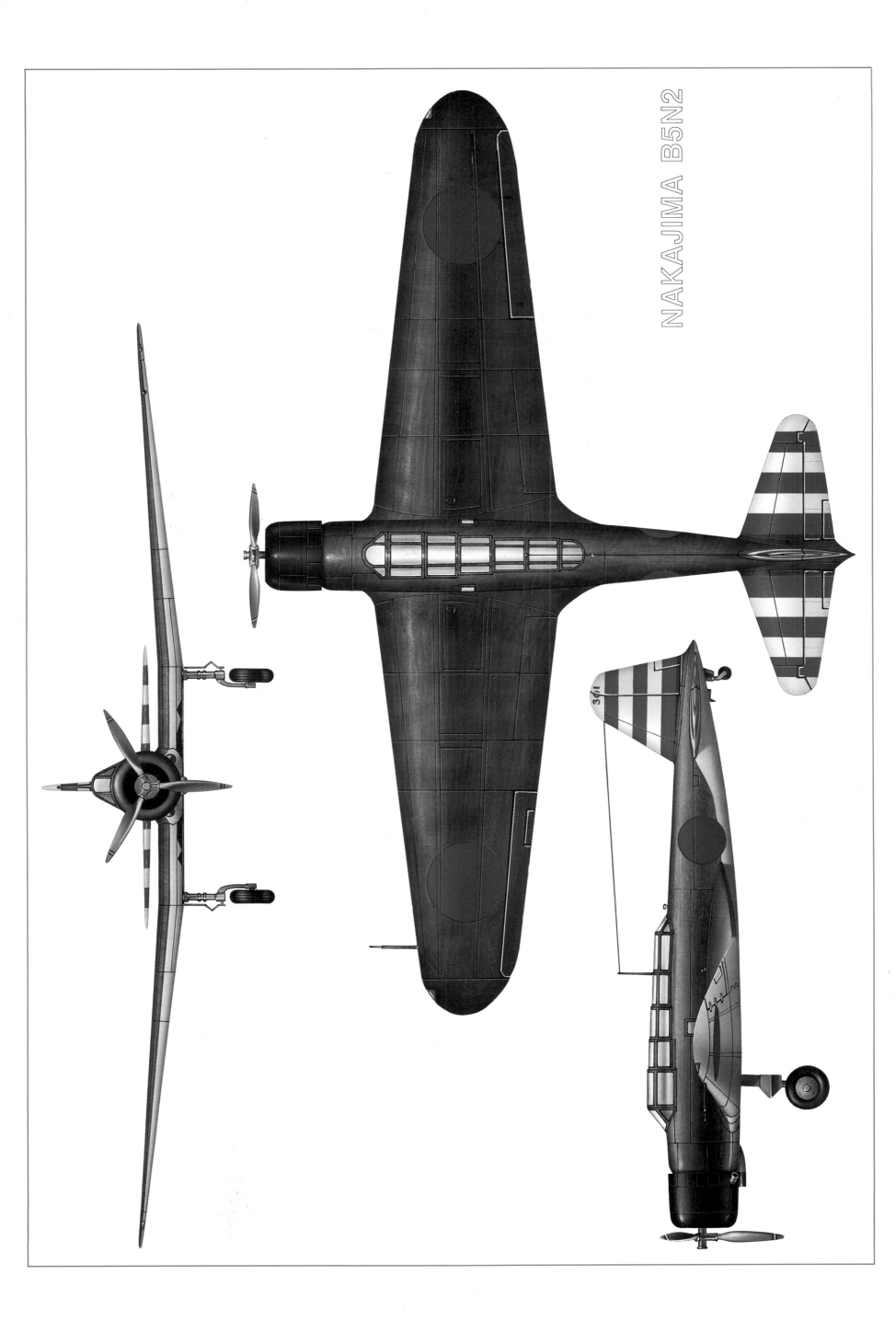

NAKAJIMA B5N2

When war broke out in the Pacific, the Imperial Navy possessed one of the most modern carrier-based torpedo planes in the world at the time, the Nakajima B5N. Known as KATE in the Allies' identification code, this large single-engine aircraft made its debut in combat on the day of Pearl Harbor. Its extensive operational career came to an end in 1944. Between 1937 and 1943, a total of 1,149 of these torpedo planes were built in two principal series.

Nakajima prepared the prototype on the basis of specifications issued by the Imperial Navy in 1935, requesting a carrier-based bomber to replace the Yokosuka B4Y1. The project was executed by a team headed by Katsuji Nakamura. The specifications called for a monoplane with a wingspan no greater than 52 ft (16 m) — to be reduced to a maximum of 25 ft (7.50 m) when the wings were folded — and capable of carrying a 1,764 lb (800 kg) torpedo or equivalent bomb load. Moreover, it was to be able to fly at 206 mph (333 km/h) at 6,580 ft (2,000 m) and to be provided with a range of four to seven hours at cruising speed.

The prototype, powered by a 770 hp Nakajima Hikari 3 engine, made its maiden flight in January 1937, and, during flight tests and evaluations, it more than fulfilled the requirements. After a series of minor modifications (including the replacement of the hydraulic system for folding back the half-wings by a manual one), the aircraft was preferred to its rival, designed by Mitsubishi, and it immediately went into production.

The first variant was the B5N1, which made its operational debut in China (it was used in the role of conventional bomber, among others), where it achieved notable success. These combat experiences, together with the appearance of more modern Soviet fighters in the same theater of war, led to a second variant being developed in 1939. This was much improved and provided with a more powerful engine. In fact, the major differences consisted in the fitting of the 1,000 hp Nakajima Sakae engine and in a series of modifications to the aerodynamics of the aircraft. This version, designated B5N2, went into production in 1940 and began to reach the units at the end of the year. By the time of the attack on Pearl Harbor, the new Nakajima torpedo plane had entirely replaced its predecessor in the front-line units. On December 7, 1941, the day of the attack on the American naval base, 144 B5N2s took part in the operation and contributed to its success in a decisive way. For almost three years, these aircraft were among the best in their category and took part in all air-sea operations. One of their most notable successes was the mission carried out against the aircraft carriers USS *Yorktown, Lexington*, and *Hornet*, which sank as a consequence of the precise and deadly attacks of the B5N2s.

It was not until 1944, when they were faced with new and more effective Allied aircraft, that the Nakajima torpedo planes were

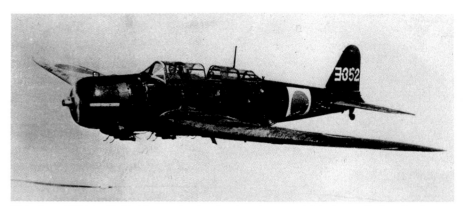

Nakajima B5N in flight. The racks for the bombs are visible beneath the fuselage.

withdrawn from front-line service and assigned to land-based units. This did not mean that they became any less effective, and they performed admirably in the role of antisubmarine convoy escort. Initially reconnaissance was entirely visual, but later some KATEs were fitted with radar equipment (the antenna being installed on the sides of the fuselage and along the leading edges of the wings) and magnetic detectors. In the last months of the war, many B5N2s were relegated to training duty (flanking the special B5N1-K aircraft derived from the first production version for this purpose), and target and glider-towing.

---

color plate

Nakajima B5N2 Imperial Japanese Navy Air Force. Commander Mitsuo Fuchida's personal aircraft, from which he led the attack on Pearl Harbor on December 7, 1941.

Aircraft:	Nakajima B5N2
Nation:	Japan
Manufacturer:	Nakajima Hikoki KK
Type:	Torpedo-bomber
Year:	1940
Engine:	Nakajima NK1B Sakae 11, 14-cylinder radial, air-cooled, 1,000 hp
Wingspan:	50 ft 11 in (15.51 m)
Length:	33 ft 9 1/2 in (10.30 m)
Height:	12 ft (3.70 m)
Weight:	9,039 lb (4,108 kg) loaded
Maximum speed:	235 mph (378 km/h) at 11,810 ft (3,600 m)
Ceiling:	27,100 ft (8,260 m)
Range:	1,237 miles (2,000 km)
Armament:	1 machine gun; 1 x 1,764 lb (800 kg) torpedo
Crew:	3

The first wave of Japanese bombers during the dramatic moment of takeoff from the aircraft carrier *Akagi* at dawn on December 7, 1941 for the attack on Pearl Harbor. Fifteen Nakajima KATE bombers and 12 KATE torpedo bombers took off from the *Akagi*.

JAPAN

The Japanese attack followed that carried out by Hitler by just over two years, but was no less devastating. On the day of the events at Pearl Harbor, the modernity and potential of the Empire of the Rising Sun's navy and air force were revealed for the first time, as was their remarkable efficiency. This fact influenced the first six months of the war in the Pacific, and faced with an adversary that proved to be increasingly fierce and powerful, the Allies in general and the United States in particular were subsequently forced to make an enormous effort to gain supremacy in the air.

In 1939, the true extent of the Empire of the Rising Sun's rearmament was still little known in the West, despite the worrying signs emerging from the conflict with China. Above all, the aeronautical potential that Japan had succeeded in developing in the years immediately prior to World War II was underestimated. Apart from the remarkably high quality of its aircraft, Japan's main strength lay in an extremely advanced industrial network that was almost entirely oriented toward military production and that proceeded in perfect harmony with the dynamism of the army and the navy and with their great need to strengthen their respective air forces.

The aeronautical production figures in the three years that immediately preceded Japan's entry into the war are the clearest indication of how intensive preparation for the conflict was: 3,201 aircraft constructed in 1938, followed by 4,467 in 1939, and by 4,768 in 1940. The increase in production was accompanied by a further strengthening of the industrial network, which was thus able to develop its immense potential to the full. In 1941, in particular, 5,080 aircraft of all types came off the assembly lines (including 1,080 fighters and 1,461 bombers). Moreover, in the same year, production of propellers and aircraft engines totaled 12,621 and 12,151 respectively.

Thus, when the war broke out in the Pacific, everything was ready. The Imperial army air force had approximately 1,500 aircraft ready for service at its disposal, and it was entrusted with the responsibility of missions carried out mainly on land. Although it had an almost similar number of aircraft at its disposal (1,400 front-line aircraft), the navy air force was given a rather more difficult task, at least in the initial phase of the conflict: to neutralize the American fleet by means of the carrier-based aircraft and, subsequently, to back the conquest of islands in the Pacific with the land-based units. After Pearl Harbor and up to the second half of 1942, both air forces carried out their respective duties successfully, and the continuous series of victories nourished the myth of Japanese invincibility. The turning point was reached in the great air-sea battles of the spring and summer of 1942, especially the Battle of Midway.

Chronology

1940

August. The Nakajima Ki-44 fighter makes its first flight in Japan, destined for the Imperial Navy. Designated Tojo, it went into service in September 1942, and a total of 1,225 aircraft were built in three basic versions. The Ki-44 was widely used against the B-29 air raids on Japan.

1941

January. The Kawanishi H8K1, a seaplane with a remarkable range, takes to the air. It was the final version of a project that originated in 1933. This large four-engine aircraft was one of the most effective in its category to be used in combat by the Japanese, and 215 were built between 1938 and 1942. The Kawanishi H8K1 proved to be extremely efficient in the role of naval reconnaissance.

December. Flight testing begins on the prototype of the Kawasaki Ki-61 Hien, the only Japanese fighter to be fitted with an in-line liquid-cooled engine (a Daimler Benz DB 601A built on license). A total of 3,078 were built in four main versions that came off the assembly lines between August 1942 and August 1945. It went into service in February 1943 and was to serve for the entire duration of the war. However, although it was generally effective, this fighter never proved to be very competitive.

HANDLEY PAGE HALIFAX Mk.III

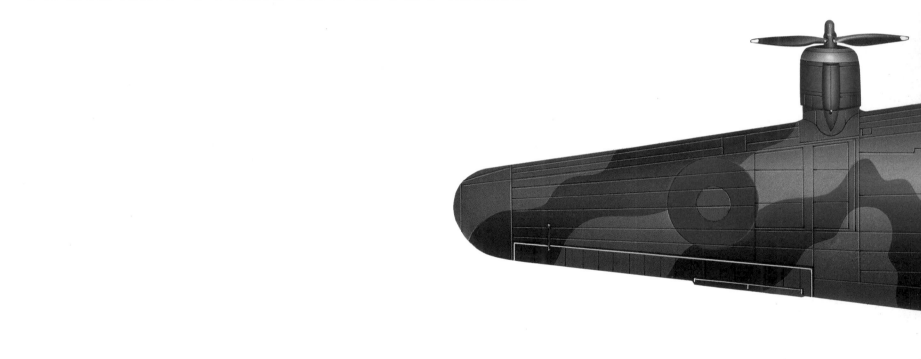

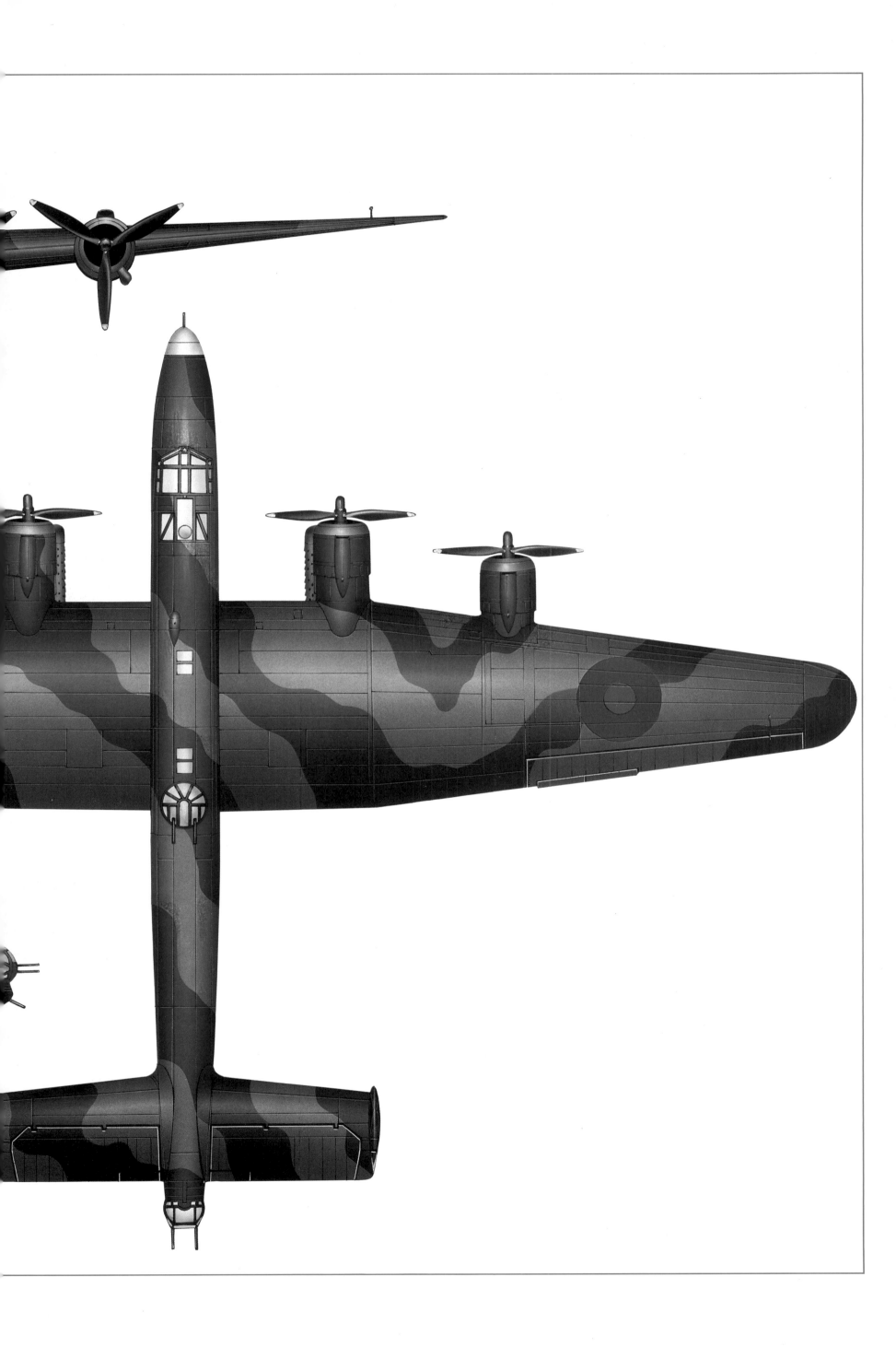

The Royal Air Force's second heavy bomber, the Handley Page Halifax, went into service only three months after the Short Stirling. However, despite this brief space of time, the new aircraft proved to be greatly superior to the previous one. This was due not only to its overall performance, which classified the Halifax as one of the best combat planes of its kind in the entire war, but also to its remarkable versatility, in addition to the role of night bomber, the large four-engine aircraft was used successfully in the roles of transport plane, air ambulance, glider-tower and naval reconnaissance. In all, 6,176 aircraft in a dozen production series came off the assembly lines, and after having been in service from November 1940 until the end of the war, the last of them were not withdrawn until the beginning of 1952. An idea of the importance of the Halifax's operative career in the events of the war can be appreciated with the help of a few figures: from March 11, 1941 (date of the first bombing raid carried out on Le Havre by the aircraft in service with the 35th Squadron of Bomber Command) to April 25, 1945, the four-engine Handley Pages carried out no fewer than 75,532 missions and dropped more than 227,000 tons of bombs on European targets. This career was obscured only by that of the aircraft's direct successor, the Avro Lancaster, the best of the trio of British strategic bombers.

The project for the Halifax originated on the basis of specifications issued by the British Air Ministry in 1935, requesting the creation of a two-engine bomber. Handley Page responded to this request with a project (HP 55) that was rejected. A year later, in September 1936, a second set of specifications was issued, regarding a medium-heavy bomber that was to be powered by a pair of Rolls-Royce Vulture engines that were being developed at the time. Once again, Handley Page responded and its project (HP 56) was judged valid. Subsequently, the project was substantially revised, with the adoption of four Rolls-Royce Merlin engines being foreseen. The construction of two prototypes (HP 57) was authorized on September 3, 1937, and the first of these took to the air on October 25, 1939. Compared to the original specifications, the new aircraft was much larger, and its total weight had more than doubled.

The first Halifax of the initial Mk.I series took to the air almost a year later, on October 11, 1940. It was an all-metal mid-wing monoplane powered by four Rolls-Royce Merlin X engines, each generating 1,280 hp and driving three-bladed variable-pitch metal propellers. The defensive armament consisted of six machine guns, two in a nose turret and four in a rear position; the bomb load totaled 13,000 lb (5,890 kg) and was completely housed inside the fuselage. Following the construction of 2,050 Mk.I and Mk.II series aircraft (the latter was provided with more powerful engines and armament and was characterized by a substantial improvement in performance), toward the middle of 1943, the Mk.III, the second major production variant, appeared and with it the Halifax underwent a radical change: in place of the four liquid-cooled Rolls-Royce engines, Bristol Hercules XVI radials were installed, each generating 1,615 hp. The Halifax Mk.III went into service in February 1944, and 2,060 were built. The final bomber versions were the Mk.VI and Mk.VII, characterized by the adoption of more powerful engines and overall improvements, especially as far as range was concerned.

Among the series not realized for land bombing, mention should be made of the Mk.V, destined for Coastal Command, and the Mk.VII, used for launching paratroops. Immediately after the war, two other variants were built for this particular role: the Mk. VIII (more than 100) and the Mk.IX (approximately 400).

color plate

Handley Page Halifax Mk.III 158th Bomber Squadron Royal Air Force - Lissett, Yorkshire, Great Britain 1945.
One of the four Halifax that exceeded 100 war missions, carrying out 128 raids

Aircraft:	Handley Page Halifax Mk.I
Nation:	Great Britain
Manufacturer:	Handley Page Ltd.
Type:	Bomber
Year:	1940
Engine:	4 Rolls-Royce Merlin X, 12-cylinder V, liquid-cooled, 1,280 hp each
Wingspan:	98 ft 10 in (30.12 m)
Length:	70 ft 1 in (21.36 m)
Height:	20 ft 9 in (6.33 m)
Weight:	55,000 lb (24,947 kg) loaded
Maximum speed:	265 mph (426 km/h) at 17,500 ft (5,300 m)
Ceiling:	22,800 ft (6,950 km)
Range:	1,860 miles (3,000 km)
Armament:	6 machine guns; 13,000 lb (5,890 kg) of bombs
Crew:	7

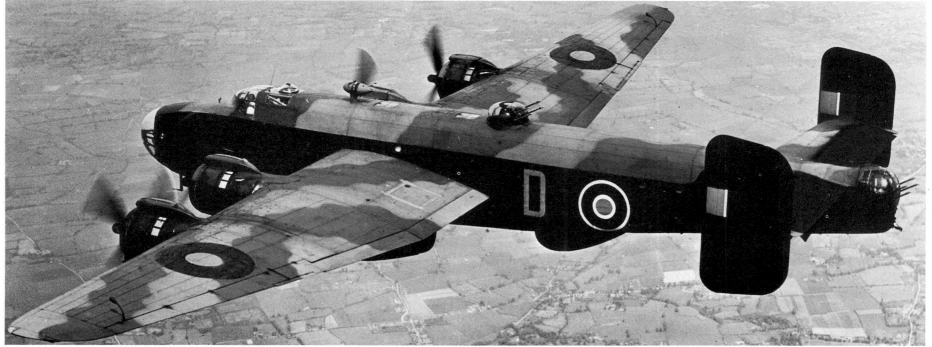

A Handley Page Halifax Mk.III with fuselage roundels and fin flashes of the type used in the final stages of the war.

KAWASAKI Ki-45

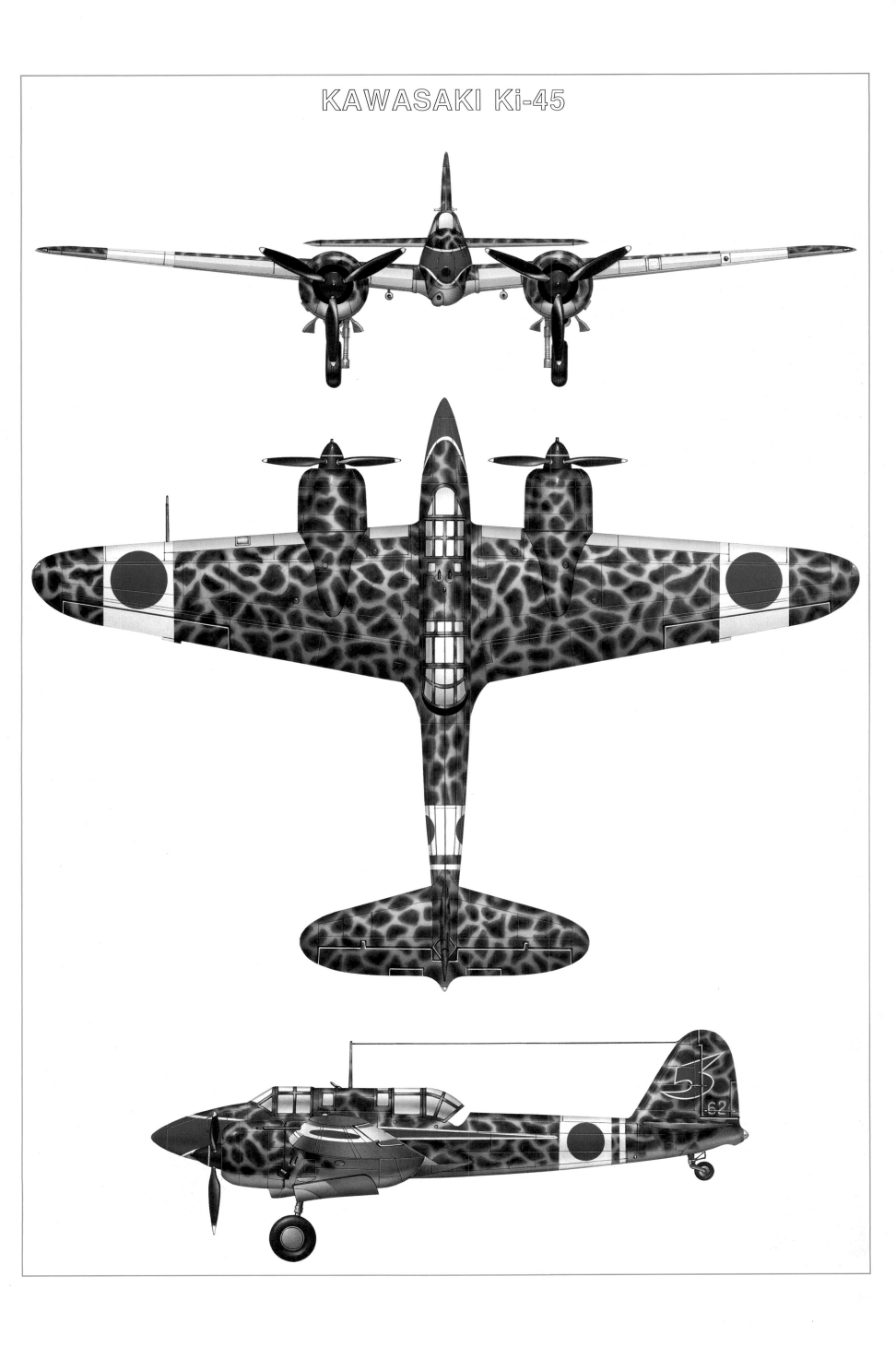

Ki-45 of the 53rd Sentai, a special ramming unit.

The tendency to build two-engine heavy fighters, present in the air forces of the major powers during the 1930s, was also to have a strong influence in Japan. In the spring of 1937, Imperial Army authorities issued specifications for a combat plane of this type, suitable for long-range missions. The result was the Kawasaki Ki-45, an aircraft that, like its Western counterparts, did not prove to be effective in the role for which it had originally been conceived, but, after having carried out a variety of duties, eventually found its true dimension as a night fighter. Between August 1941 and July 1945, a total of 1,701 Ki-45s were completed in several versions that remained in service for almost the entire duration of the conflict. In the last months of the war, during the Japaneses' desperate attempts to defend their country, the Ki-45s of the final production series fought extremely hard (and to great effect) to combat the massive night raids of the American Boeing B-29s.

The Imperial Navy's specifications for the new aircraft were remarkably precise. Some of the most notable requests included a maximum speed of 335 mph (540 km/h) at 11,515 ft (3,500 m), an operational ceiling between 6,580 ft (2,000 m) and 16,450 ft (5,000 m), a range of four hours and 40 minutes at 217 mph (350 km/h) plus a further half hour at full power. The three largest aeronautical manufacturers (Nakajima, Mitsubishi, and Kawasaki) all submitted projects but, toward the end of 1937, authorization to procede with the development of the project was granted to Kawasaki, and this task was carried out by Takeo Doi. Work on the prototype began in January 1938, and exactly one year later the first aircraft, designated Ki-38, took to the air for the first time.

This date marked the beginning of a long and tormented development phase that lasted almost two and a half years and led to the aircraft being substantially modified. The prototype was a cantilever mid-wing monoplane with retractable landing gear and was originally powered by two 820 hp Nakajima Ha-20B radial engines. The disappointing performance of the engines created the first set of problems, subsequently made worse by a series of difficulties of an aerodynamic nature caused mainly by the engine nacelles. Flight testing was suspended in the second half of 1939 in order to study solutions to these setbacks. The initial solutions involved fitting more powerful engines, but radical redesigning of the whole aircraft went ahead for a long time. The first of the three definitive prototypes did not appear until May 1941, and the optimum configuration was achieved in the subsequent 12 preseries aircraft. Following these modifications, the two-engine

Kawasaki was redesignated Ki-45 KAIa (KAI being the abbreviation for Kaizo, modified).

In Japan, the Ki-45 was ambitiously christened *Toryu* (Dragon-Killer), although in the Allies' code it was known by the more banal name of NICK, and it went into service in August 1942, initially being used as a ground-attack aircraft and in antishipping duty. Combat experiences (especially in the latter role) led to a second variant being developed. This was the Ki-45 KAIb, fitted with more powerful armament: one 20 mm and one 37 mm cannon were installed in the nose, replacing the two 12.7 mm machine guns and the 20 mm cannon in the belly of the first production series aircraft. However, the 7.92 mm flexible machine gun in the observer's position was retained. The armament was further improved in the next major production series (the Ki-45 KAIc of 1943, a total of 477 being built), with the installation of a pair of 20 mm cannons on the aircraft's back, so that they could fire upward at an angle in a similar way to those tested on German night fighters. These aircraft proved to be very efficient and, although they were not provided with radar, they proved to be an effective weapon against American air raids on Japan.

color plate

Kawasaki Ki-45 53rd Sentai Japanese Imperial Army Air Force - Japan 1944

Aircraft:	Kawasaki Ki-45 KAIa
Nation:	Japan
Manufacturer:	Kawasaki Kokuki Kogyo KK
Type:	Fighter
Year:	1941
Engine:	2 Nakajima Ha-25,14-cylinder radial, air-cooled, 1,050 hp each
Wingspan:	49 ft 3 in (15.02 m)
Length:	34 ft 9 in (10.60 m)
Height:	12 ft 2 in (3.70 m)
Weight:	12,081 lb (5,491 kg) loaded
Maximum speed:	340 mph (547 km/h) at 22,965 ft (7,000 m)
Ceiling:	35,200 ft (10,730 m)
Range:	1,404 miles (2,260 km)
Armament:	1 × 20 mm cannon; 3 machine guns; 1,100 lb (500 kg) of bombs
Crew:	2

MITSUBISHI Ki-51

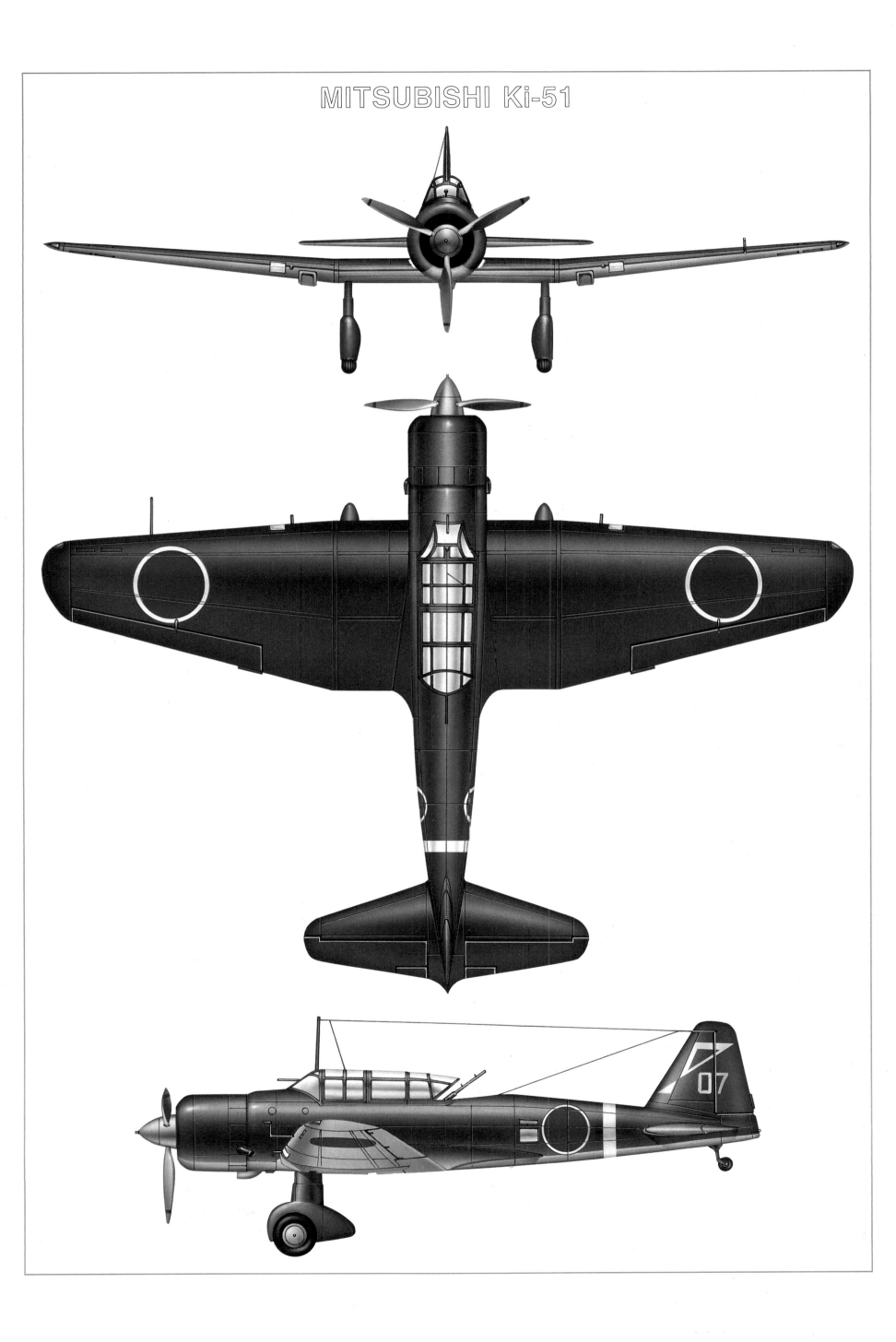

The Mitsubishi Ki-51 was the Imperial Army air force's true "all-rounder." Conceived in 1938 as a ground-attack plane and overtaken by more modern aircraft in the course of the conflict, it was never withdrawn from front-line duty, thanks to excellent features, including sturdiness, reliability, and maneuverability, that made it practically irreplaceable in tactical roles. The overall effectiveness of the project is demonstrated by the fact that the Ki-51 (christened SONIA in the Allies' identification code) remained virtually unaltered throughout the long period in which it was produced. In fact production commenced in 1940 and ceased in July 1945 and amounted to no fewer than 2,385 aircraft.

In 1937 Imperial Army authorities issued the specifications that were to lead to the creation of the Ki-51. These requested a ground-attack plane derived from the earlier Ki-30 light bomber, but more agile and compact. Great emphasis was placed on maneuverability, on protection for the crew, and on the possibility of operating from emergency airstrips located near the combat area. As for the aircraft's performance, its maximum speed was to be no less than 260 mph (420 km/h) at 6,578 ft (2,000 m), takeoff weight was to be 5,960 lb (2,700 kg), it was to have a bomb load of 440 lb (200 kg) and defensive armament consisting of three machine guns, one of which was to be movable.

The Mitsubishi project was entrusted to the same team that had designed the Ki-30, Kawano, Ohki, and Mizuno, and the first two prototypes were completed in the summer of 1939. These were followed by 11 preseries aircraft that were used for evaluation tests, during which their already remarkable characteristics were further improved through modifications of an aerodynamic nature.

The Ki-51 was an all-metal low-wing monoplane with fixed and faired landing gear, and it was characterized by the long glazed cockpit that housed the pilot and the observer-gunner. The latter had a 7.7 mm machine gun fitted onto a movable mounting at his disposal for the defense of the rear, while the rest of the defensive armament consisted of two similar weapons (subsequently replaced by two 12.7 mm machine guns) which were fixed and installed on the wings. The power plant was a 940 hp Mitsubishi Ha-26 II radial engine.

The aircraft made its operational debut in China, and when Japan entered World War II, it was widely used in the Pacific, equipping almost all the operative units. In 1944, the continually growing demand, and the need to satisfy it, led to the opening of a new assembly line at the Tachikawa Dai-Ichi Rikugun Kokusho (Tachikawa Army Air Force Arsenal), which built no fewer than 913 aircraft. Thus, the Ki-51's career continued until the end of the war, when the final role assigned it was that of suicide plane.

Attempts to develop a more powerful version of the SONIA were not lacking. In 1941 Mitsubishi prepared three prototypes for use in tactical reconnaissance and designated Ki-71. These aircraft were provided with more powerful engines and with retractable landing gear. However, the improvements were not satisfactory enough to justify their going into production.

---

color plate

Mitsubishi Ki-51 44th Sentai Japanese Imperial Army Air Force - China 1942

Above, final control before takeoff; note the bombs under the wings. Below, a formation of Ki-51s employed by the 44th Sentai. Above right, a Ki-51 with landing gear lacking fairing and with the modified spinner characteristic of the last models to be built.

Aircraft:	Mitsubishi Ki-51
Nation:	Japan
Manufacturer:	Mitsubishi Jukogyo KK
Type:	Attack
Year:	1940
Engine:	Mitsubishi Ha-26 II, 14-cylinder radial, air-cooled, 940 hp
Wingspan:	39 ft 8 1/2 in (12.10 m)
Length:	30 ft 2 1/2 in (9.21 m)
Height:	8 ft 11 1/2 in (2.73 m)
Weight:	6,415 lb (2,915 kg) loaded
Maximum speed:	263 mph (424 km/h) at 9,840 ft (3,000 m)
Ceiling:	27,130 ft (8,270 m)
Range:	660 miles (1,060 km)
Armament:	3 machine guns; 440 lb (200 kg) of bombs
Crew:	2

GREAT BRITAIN

Hitler's renouncement of Operation Sea Lion and the subsequent conclusion of the Battle of Britain made the launching of the second stage in the strengthening and modernization of the British air force possible. The direct clash with the powerful adversary had been violent and had galvanized all the nation's energy: from August 13, 1940 until October 31, the fighting raged unceasingly, with the ratio of strength clearly in favor of the Luftwaffe: 3,550 German aircraft (2,000 bombers, 600 of which were dive-bombers, 1,250 fighters, 300 reconnaissance planes) were in operation throughout August, against just over 1,000 Hurricanes and Spitfires. In the end, the Royal Air Force lost 915 aircraft, compared to 1,733 belonging to the enemy, although in return it had also been able to verify its great vitality and the solidity of the tactical and strategical theories that lay at the basis of its formation.

Under the guidance of General Hugh Trenchard, in the years immediately prior to the war, the RAF had become the only air force in Europe capable of withstanding the German Luftwaffe. As far as its aircraft were concerned, the Hawker Hurricane, its first modern monoplane fighter, had been in service since 1937, and the British were preparing to introduce the Supermarine Spitfire. As for its bombers, the most representative aircraft were the two-engine Bristol Blenheim, Handley Page Hampden, Vickers Wellington, and Armstrong Whitworth Whitley.

However, the strengthening did not concern only the aircraft and operative organization. The priority given to defending national territory and the virtual certainty that this would be among the first targets of a German attack had led to the creation, from 1935 onward, of a chain of radar stations along the southern coast of England. In July 1939, this network consisted of 20 such stations, capable of spotting aircraft at a distance of 60-125 miles (100-200 km) away at altitudes over 9,870 ft (3,000 m) and of communicating information about their course to central command.

The end of the direct threat to national territory thus made a more efficient distribution of energy possible and, consequently, the aeronautical industry was also able to be strengthened further, in order to face the growing requests for increasingly effective aircraft that came from theaters of war all over the world. The RAF's most prestigious aircraft originated during this period: the Bristol Beaufighter, the de Havilland Mosquito, the increasingly powerful versions of the Spitfire, great strategic bombers such as the Short Stirling, the Handley Page Halifax and the Avro Lancaster. In fact, from 1940, all efforts were concentrated on these aircraft. Moreover, the need to carry out increasingly intensive and effective bombing raids on a Europe dominated by the Germans had become a priority in order to weaken the formidable German war machine.

Aeronautical production was at an extremely high level and proved capable of adapting constantly to the increasing demands made upon it: in 1938, a total of 4,000 aircraft were built, and this increased to 7,000 in 1939, to 15,000 in 1940, and to 20,100 in 1941.

Chronology

1940

February 24. The prototype of the Hawker Typhoon takes to the air. The aircraft was to go into service in 1941 and proved to be an excellent ground-attack plane.

October 11. The first production series four-engine Handley Page Halifax takes to the air. It was the second major British bomber of the war, and a total of 6,176 were built.

November 25. Flight testing of the prototype of the de Havilland DH 98 Mosquito, one of the most famous and widely used British aircraft of the entire war. Between 1941 and 1950, a total of 6,439 were built in dozens of versions, while a further 1,342 were built in Australia and Canada.

1941

January 9. The prototype of the Avro Lancaster makes its maiden flight. Derived from the airframe of the two-engine Manchester, this bomber was the most famous of its kind to be used in combat by the RAF, and from the end of 1941 until the early months of 1946, a total of 7,366 were built.

February 10-11. The four-engine bomber Short Stirling makes its operational debut in a night raid on Rotterdam. The Stirling was the first in its category to go into service in the units of the RAF, and although it never achieved the fame of the Halifax or the Lancaster, it was used for the entire duration of the conflict.

May 15. The first British aircraft to be powered by a jet engine makes its maiden flight. This was the experimental prototype Gloster E 28/39, fitted with a Whittle W.1 engine with 860 lb (390 kg) thrust, and it was tested with success. The first British jet fighter, the Gloster Meteor, was derived from it.

June 29. The second prototype of the Fairey Barracuda torpedo plane takes to the air. A total of 2,572 aircraft in several production series were derived from this definitive configuration. They went into service in January 1943 and remained operative throughout the war. Some aircraft remained in service with the Fleet Air Arm until 1953.

December 22. The prototype of the Fairey Firefly carrier-based fighter makes its maiden flight. The aircraft went into service in October 1943 and was used mainly in the Pacific. The last of the Mk.I series (950 of which were built) remained in use until the end of 1946.

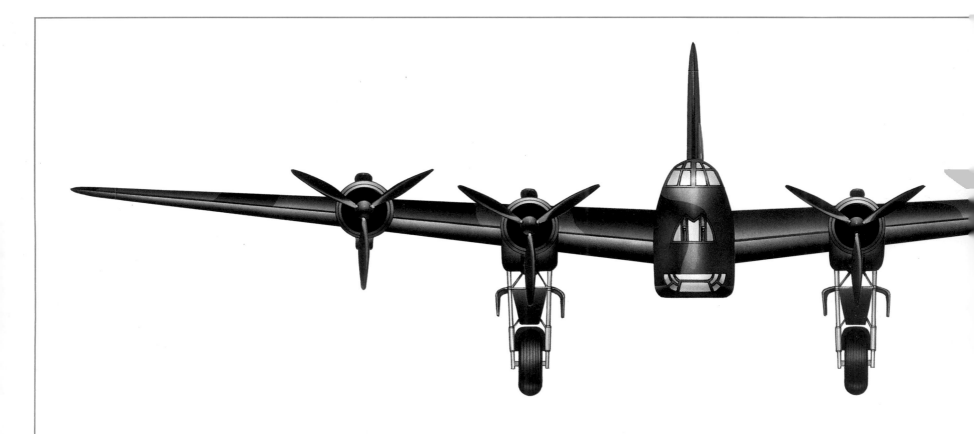

SHORT STIRLING Mk.I

Among the countries involved in the conflict, Great Britain was the first to feel the need for a four-engine heavy bomber. The first aircraft of this type was the Short Stirling, although, unlike its successors, the Handley Page Halifax and the Avro Lancaster, it did not prove to be particularly effective in the role for which it had been conceived, especially as far as its performance at high altitude was concerned. Nevertheless, the Stirling remained in front-line service until the middle of 1943, when it was gradually used for less important missions and relegated to secondary roles, such as transport and glider-towing, for which the last two production series, the Mk.IV and the Mk.V, were purposely built. A total of 2,371 aircraft in four major production versions came off the assembly lines.

The Stirling originated in 1936, when the British Air Ministry issued specifications for a heavy bomber with a seven- or eight-man crew. Short traditionally specialized in the construction of seaplanes, and the Stirling was its first large land aircraft with retractable landing gear. Its designers therefore preferred to study suitable solutions on a reduced-scale model before building the actual prototype. Designated Short S.31 and powered by four 91 hp Pobjoy Niagara engines, this experimental aircraft was a half-scale version of the four-engine aircraft. It was flown for the first time in great secrecy on September 19, 1938 and the experiences that followed were considered extremely useful as far as the development of the real project was concerned. Nevertheless, following its maiden flight on May 14, 1939, the first "real" prototype, the Short S.29 Stirling, was totally destroyed while landing. It was therefore necessary to build a second experimental aircraft with which to complete the series of flight tests and evaluations. The aircraft went into production sometime after and the first Stirling Mk.I took to the air on May 7, 1940. Three months later, deliveries to the units of Bomber Command commenced, and the aircraft made its operational debut on the night of February 10-11, 1941 in an air raid on Rotterdam.

This mission was the first of a long series of bombing attacks, first in daylight and then solely at night, in which the Short Stirling was used until the more effective Halifax and Lancaster bombers became available in greater numbers. In fact, the Stirling had an insufficient operative ceiling (mainly due to its wings being too short, although this had specifically been requested by the Air Ministry at the start so that the aircraft would fit existing hangars), and it was incapable of carrying large, high-potency bombs. It carried out its last mission in the units of Bomber Command on September 8, 1944, although halfway through the previous year the Stirling had virtually been withdrawn from front-line duty, gradually being assigned to glider-towing and transport.

In 1942, the initial production series was followed by aircraft of the Mk.III variant, which featured heavier armament, with a new type of turret on the aircraft's back, and more powerful engines, the 1,650 hp Hercules XVI. Previously, the construction of a version built on license in Canada had been planned. This was designated Mk.II and fitted with American Wright-Cyclone R-2600 engines, but only very few had been completed. The next series, the Mk.IV, was developed specifically for glider-towing: deprived of two-thirds of its defensive armament and provided with the appropriate equipment, it proved to be very effective, and the 450 aircraft of this type built took part in all the major operations during the last two years of the conflict, making their debut on June 6, 1944, during the Allied invasion of Normandy. The last Stirlings to be built were 160 Mk.Vs that were transformed into transport planes and were in service from January 1945 throughout the whole of the following year, when they were replaced by the Avro York.

color plate
Short Stirling Mk.I 7th Bomber Squadron Royal Air Force - Oakington, Great Britain 1941

Aircraft:	Short Stirling Mk.I
Nation:	Great Britain
Manufacturer:	Short Brothers Ltd.
Type:	Bomber
Year:	1940
Engine:	4 Bristol Hercules XI, 14-cylinder radial, air-cooled, 1,590 hp each
Wingspan:	99 ft 1 in (30.21 m)
Length:	87 ft 3 in (26.60 m)
Height:	22 ft 9 in (6.93 m)
Weight:	59,400 lb (26,943 kg) loaded
Maximum speed:	260 mph (418 km/h) at 10,500 ft (3,200 m)
Ceiling:	17,000 ft (5,180 m)
Range:	2,330 miles (3,750 km)
Armament:	8 machine guns; 14,000 lb (6,350 kg) of bombs
Crew:	7-8

A Short Stirling Mk.III adopted by the 214th Squadron of the Royal Air Force.

BRISTOL BEAUFORT

BRISTOL BEAUFORT

As well as the effective Beaufighter, another aircraft built by the Bristol company had long been the standard torpedo plane in service in the Royal Air Force's Coastal Command. This was the Beaufort, a sturdy and fast aircraft that for three years (from 1940 to 1943) carried out its role in an excellent manner, being used mainly in the North Sea, the Atlantic and the Mediterranean. Total production in Great Britain amounted to 1,121 aircraft in two series, characterized mainly by the adoption of different types of engine. To these were added a further 700 aircraft built in Australia.

The specifications that gave rise to the Beaufort were issued by the British Air Ministry in 1935. There were two distinct requests: the first for a monoplane torpedo aircraft powered by two Bristol Perseus radial engines; the second for a bomber reconnaissance aircraft. Both sets of specifications were fulfilled by Bristol with the creation of derivatives from the excellent project that had led to the Type 142 Blenheim: the first with the development of the Type 152, the second with the Type 149 Bolingbroke, which was built in Canada.

Work on the Type 152 began in the summer of 1936, on the basis of an initial contract for 78 production series aircraft, and the prototype of the Beaufort took to the air for the first time on October 15, 1938. It was an all-metal mid-wing monoplane that closely resembled the Blenheim Mk.IV, retaining its layout and general structure. The main difference lay in the fuselage, which was noticeably higher and ended in a turret on its back provided with two machine guns. Another turret, provided with two similar weapons, was situated in the front part of the nose. The offensive armament consisted of a 1,325 lb (600 kg) bomb load, although this could be increased to 1,986 lb (900 kg) in exceptional circumstances, or a 1,611 lb (730 kg) torpedo. It was powered by a pair of Bristol Taurus 14-cylinder radial engines, whose potential increased from 1,010 hp in the initial production series aircraft to 1,130 hp in the subsequent ones. The change to this power plant instead of the one planned originally was made necessary by the remarkable increase in weight (approximately 25 percent) that occurred during the development of the project.

The new engines actually contributed to slowing down preparation of the aircraft, already hampered by many problems. In fact, the series of flight tests and operative evaluations was particularly long, and it was not until the beginning of 1940 that the first Beaufort Mk.Is (955 built in all) began to equip the 22nd Squadron of Coastal Command. The aircraft's operational debut took place on the night of April 15-16, with a mine-laying mission.

Production went ahead with the Beaufort Mk.II, in which 1,200 hp American Pratt & Whitney Twin Wasp radial engines were adopted. The first of the 166 built took to the air in September 1941. Two other versions were proposed but never followed up: the Mk.III, with a pair of 1,280 hp Rolls-Royce Merlin XX engines,

A Beaufort employed by the Kemley Station Flight.

and the Mk.IV, with two 1,267 hp Bristol Taurus XX engines.

The adoption of American engines characterized an interesting production series of Beauforts built in Australia from 1940. There were several versions, and all were entirely different due to the characteristics of the engine and the propellers: the first was the Mk.V (which took to the air in May 1941, a total of 50 being built in all), that was followed by 30 Mk.VAs, by 60 Mk.VIs, by 40 Mk.VIIs, and by 520 Mk.VIIIs. The final variant remained in production until August 1944 and was characterized by improvements to the fuel tanks, armament, and navigation system.

color plate

Bristol Beaufort 42nd Squadron Royal Air Force - Thorney Island, Great Britain 1940

Aircraft:	Bristol Beaufort Mk.I
Nation:	Great Britain
Manufacturer:	Bristol Aeroplane Co. Ltd.
Type:	Torpedo-bomber
Year:	1940
Engine:	2 Bristol Taurus VI, 14-cylinder radial, air-cooled, 1,130 hp each
Wingspan:	57 ft 10 in (17.62 m)
Length:	44 ft 7 in (13.59 m)
Height:	12 ft 5 in (3.79 m)
Weight:	21,228 lb (9,630 kg) loaded
Maximum speed:	265 mph (426 km/h) at 6,000 ft (1,800 m)
Ceiling:	16,500 ft (5,050 m)
Range:	1,600 miles (2,575 km)
Armament:	4 machine guns; 1 × 1,611 lb (730 kg) torpedo
Crew:	4

An Australian built Bristol Beaufort Mk.VI. The aircraft produced in Australia were fitted with engines made in the United States.

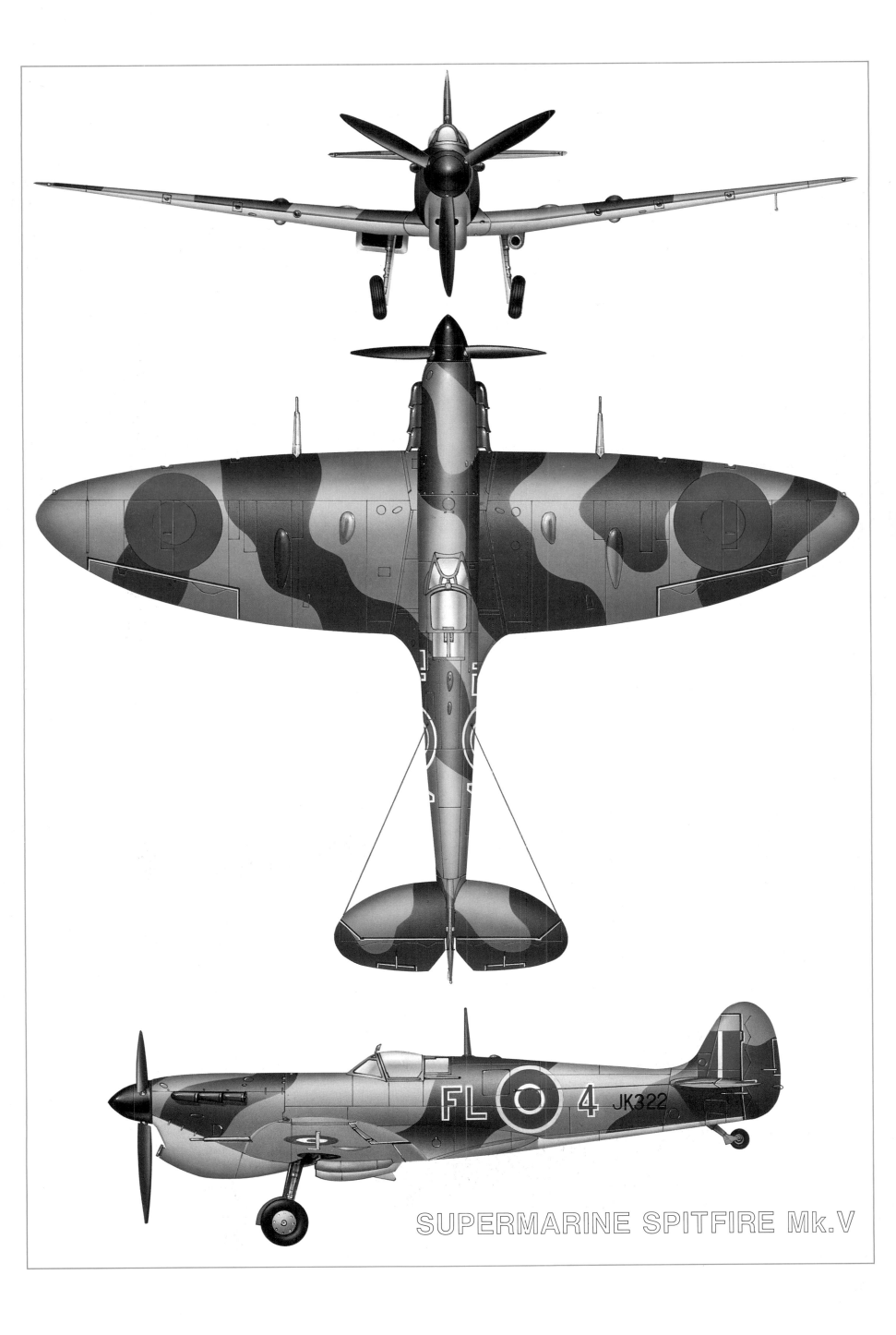

SUPERMARINE SPITFIRE Mk.V

SUPERMARINE SPITFIRE Mk.V

The evolution of the Supermarine Spitfire, the best British fighter of the conflict and among the best of those of all the nations at war, proceeded at a similar rate to that of its principal and immediate German adversaries: first, the Messerschmitt Bf.109 and subsequently the Focke Wulf Fw.190. There was a continuous search for a margin of superiority in order to conquer and retain, time after time, supremacy in the air, and the confrontation that began during the Battle of Britain went ahead without interruption for the entire duration of World War II.

Following the construction of 1,583 Spitfire Mk.Is (in service since June 1938), the assembly lines began to produce the first aircraft of the second production variant, the Mk.II. These fighters, which went into service toward the end of 1940, differed in the adoption of a 1,175 hp Rolls-Royce Merlin XII engine. Two main versions were completed: the Mk.IIA (750 aircraft), provided with eight machine guns, and the Mk.IIB (170 aircraft), armed with four machine guns and two 20 mm cannons. Although the search for greater power and heavier armament was apparent, the Spitfire Mk.IIs were still a transitional variant. In the subsequent Mk.V series, the first optimum compromise between performance, flexibility of use, and firepower was reached. In these Spitfires, (which began to come off the assembly lines in March 1941) two types of wing were adopted: a standard one, identified by the prefix F; and a shorter one that was clipped at the end (prefix LF) and particularly suited to flying at low altitudes. In addition, the aircraft's armament also became more articulated and flexible, varying from the eight machine guns of the subseries Mk.VA to the four machine guns and two 20 mm cannons of the Spitfire Mk.VB and the four 20 mm cannons of the Mk.VC. The last, in particular, was provided with a so-called universal wing, capable of housing all the possible armament configurations. As for the power plants, Merlin 45 and 50 engines were chosen, generating 1,440 hp and 1,490 hp respectively. Production of the Spitfire Mk.Vs was enormous, amounting to 94 of the Mk.VA variant, 3,923 of the MK.VB and 2,447 of the Mk.VC. In addition, 229 aircraft designated Spitfire Mk.IV were completed in the PR (photographic reconnaissance) configuration. In these aircraft the machine guns were replaced by an additional fuel tank with a capacity of 121 USgals (320 liters) on the leading edge of the wing, while two cameras were installed in the rear part of the fuselage in such a way as to be able to operate on both sides of the aircraft. Moreover, the cockpit was pressurized and, in order to improve the aircraft's aerodynamics at great altitudes, the wingspan was increased, up to 40 ft 5 in

A Spitfire Mk.V adapted for photographic reconnaissance.

(12.24 m) and was characterized by rounded wing tips.

In May 1941 the first clashes in combat with its immediate German adversary the Messerschmitt Bf.109 took place, although the Supermarine fighters always retained a slight overall advantage, except at altitudes over 19,735 ft (6,000 m). Use of the fighter rapidly spread and, in September, 27 units were equipped with Mk.VA aircraft; this figure had risen to 47 units three months later. In the meantime, production had reached remarkable levels: at the beginning of 1942 more than 1,700 Spitfire Mk.VS had been completed, and during the same year more than 3,300 aircraft were to come off the assembly lines.

The Mk.V series Spitfires were the first to be widely used overseas, from Malta in March 1942 to the Middle East and, from the beginning of 1943, in the Pacific. Moreover, these aircraft were also the first to be used as fighter-bombers, due to their being able to carry 498 lb (226 kg) of bombs.

The balance as compared to the German fighter was upset in September 1941, with the appearance of the new Focke Wulf Fw.190. During the first clashes (over France), it was evident that the Spitfire Mk.V was markedly inferior to its adversary: its only advantage lay in the fact that it was able to make tighter turns. The response to this new threat was not long in coming and arrived in July of the following year with the first Spitfire Mk.IXs, which were really a combination of the Mk.V airframe and the most powerful Merlin engine in the 1,565 hp version.

color plate

Supermarine Spitfire Mk.V tropicalized model of the 81st Fighter Squadron Royal Air Force - Sicily (Italy) 1943

Aircraft:	Supermarine Spitfire Mk.VB
Nation:	Great Britain
Manufacturer:	Supermarine Division of Vickers-Armstrong Ltd.
Type:	Fighter
Year:	1941
Engine:	Rolls-Royce Merlin 45, 12-cylinder V, liquid-cooled, 1,440 hp
Wingspan:	36 ft 10 in (11.22 m)
Length:	29 ft 11 in (9.12 m)
Height:	11 ft 5 in (3.43 m)
Weight:	6,417 lb (2,911 kg) loaded
Maximum speed:	374 mph (602 km/h) at 13,000 ft (4,000 m)
Ceiling:	37,000 ft (11,280 m)
Range:	470 miles (750 km)
Armament:	2 × 20 mm cannons; 4 machine guns
Crew:	1

A Turkish Air Force Spitfire Mk.V with tropical filter.

THE BATTLE OF BRITAIN

The Battle of Britain was the first great air encounter of World War II. Apart from purely military objectives, the confrontation between the Royal Air Force and the Luftwaffe placed the very role of the modern combat aircraft at stake, as it was conceived by the two most advanced nations in the aeronautical field at the time. It was not only men, aircraft and air forces that emerged from this long and bloody encounter as winners or losers, but also, and above all, different theories as far as air warfare was concerned. Those that lost were in fact the very ones that had guided the formation and growth of the German Luftwaffe up till then. These doctrines had been put to the test in singular circumstances, such as the Spanish Civil War and the early campaigns of World War II, and had led to a primarily tactical emphasis being placed both on the aircraft and the organization of the air force of the Third Reich. Germany learnt this lesson to its own cost, although paradoxically it never succeeded in putting this teaching into practice: for the rest of the war, the Luftwaffe continued to lack effective strategic potential. This was in spite of its increasing involvement in theaters of war all over the world, against adversaries whose strength continued to grow constantly.

Thus, as well as constituting a turning point (the first) in World War II, the Battle of Britain was also a long, bloody, and consuming testing ground that, apart from the most publicized phase that took place in the summer and autumn of 1940, actually involved the adversaries until May 1941, when Hitler finally admitted defeat and turned his attentions toward another, no less powerful antagonist, the Soviet Union.

Although August 13 and October 31, 1940, are usually considered the dates on which the Battle of Britain began and ended, historians are now unanimous in subdividing its development into five phases, considering the period between July 10 and August 7, 1940, as preparatory. During that time, the Luftwaffe was active mainly against shipping in the English Channel, with the aim of involving the British fighters in combat and thus weakening their strength.

This was in fact the initial objective of the first phase of the Battle of Britain, which formally began on August 8 and ended exactly ten days later on August 18. The first large-scale daytime raid on airports, radar stations, and buildings distributed along the southern and southeastern coasts of England took place on August 13, and this date is remembered as the official start of the battle. The Germans gave it the conventional name of *Adlertag*, or Eagle Day: a total of 1,485 aircraft were used operating in huge formations and following wave after wave. According to Winston Churchill's *Memoirs*, on August 11, just before the raid, the ratio of strength was as follows: the RAF had at its disposal 704 operative fighters, including 620 Hurricanes and Spitfires, and 350 bombers; the Luftwaffe had 933 Messerschmitt Bf.109 fighters, 375 Messerschmitt Bf.110 two-engine fighter-bombers, 346 Junkers Ju.87 Stuka dive-bombers, 1,015 Dornier, Heinkel and Junkers two-engine bombers, amounting to 2,669 aircraft in all.

The raids continued uninterruptedly day after day. The most violent occurred on August 15, when three German Luftflotte attacked British airports. On August 18, the Luftwaffe's losses amounted to 363 aircraft, as compared to 211 British aircraft. However, the German air force had not achieved its aim of wearing out the enemy fighters: in fact, the British pilots had received an order to place priority on attacking the bombers and not to become involved in combat with the enemy's interceptors. In this period, the strategic limitations of the Luftwaffe's aircraft emerged sensationally, and the effects of these limitations followed one after another: the Heinkel He.111 and Dornier Do.17 bombers, considered the best in the world, did not have a very long range and lacked any form of effective defense against the attacks of the British fighters. Consequently, the formations had to be protected continuously, before, during, and after missions, and, hampered in this way, the otherwise excellent Messerschmitt Bf.109s were unable to carry out their optimum role as interceptors, penalized above all in their range. Nor did the performance of the aircraft most publicized by Goering, such as the Junkers Ju.87 and the Messerschmitt Bf.110, prove to be any better, and in fact they were slow and vulnerable. The *Stukas*, in particular, were withdrawn from action on August 18, following serious losses.

The second phase of the Battle of Britain lasted from August 19 to September 6, 1940. This time the German strategy was different, and concentrated mainly on attacking airports and industrial targets, with the aim of destroying the RAF's forces. Tactics also changed. The aircraft no longer flew in huge formations, easy prey for the fighters, but in small groups that were heavily escorted and protected, capable of dispersing the enemy's reaction. This did not work either.

The third phase began on September 7, when 300 bombers carried out the first massive air raid on London. Goering had assumed control of the offensive personally and had ordered the commencement of global attacks on the British capital: the aim was not only that of causing panic among the population, but also that of dispersing the fighters involved in air defense, with provocative air raids being carried out by single aircraft in all areas within range. On the evening of September 7, more than 1,200 aircraft were involved in one of the greatest air encounters of the conflict, which lasted for little more than half an hour: the German attack comprised 300 bombers escorted by 600 fighters, and these released 337 tons of bombs. The climax of this phase occurred on September 15, with an extremely violent daytime raid on London, and it continued until September 26. Subsequently, and until October 5, the German pressure began to diminish, not only due to serious losses, but also to the desperate defense put up by the British, who used their entire potential in this period, in a balance that was difficult to maintain, made worse by the loss of pilots (irreplaceable in a brief space of time) and a shortage of aircraft. Between September 7 and September 30, the British losses amounted to 247 fighters, compared to 433 German aircraft.

On October 6, 1940, the fourth phase began, in which the Germans suspended the daytime attacks and concentrated on nighttime bombing raids in an attempt to reduce their losses. The bomber formations operated with the help of excellent radar equipment, but the British reaction remained strong and deadly. On October 31, Hitler realized that it was impossible to eliminate the British fighters. Since August 13 the RAF had lost 915 aircraft, compared to 1,733 of those belonging to the adversary. However, fighting continued, although without following the invasion plan that had been the initial objective.

From November 1, 1940, there was another change in tactics, with the beginning of the fifth and final phase of the Battle of Britain, which continued until May 10, 1941: strategic attacks, almost exclusively carried out at night, directed against industrial centers. The aim of this was to paralyze production. All the major British industrial centers were attacked; the largest and most devasting raid took place at Coventry on November 14. London also suffered raids almost nightly. The last of these occurred on the night of May 10-11, 1941, and more than 500 bombers took part. However, in the end, even this violent effort proved unsuccessful. Germany abandoned the match against its most direct adversary and turned its attention to other fronts. The course of World War II had changed direction.

NORTH AMERICAN B-25B

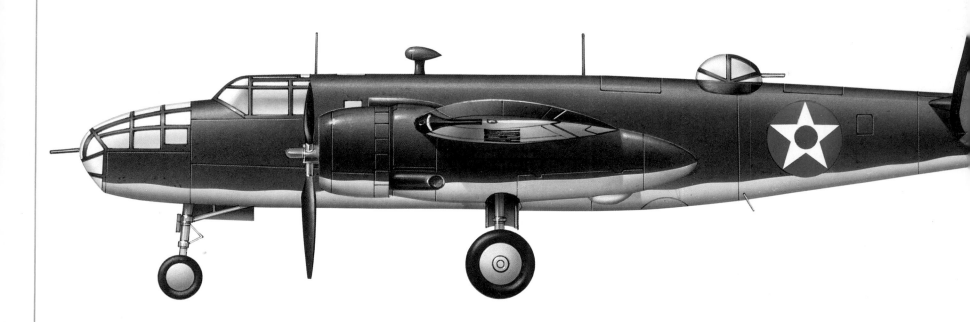

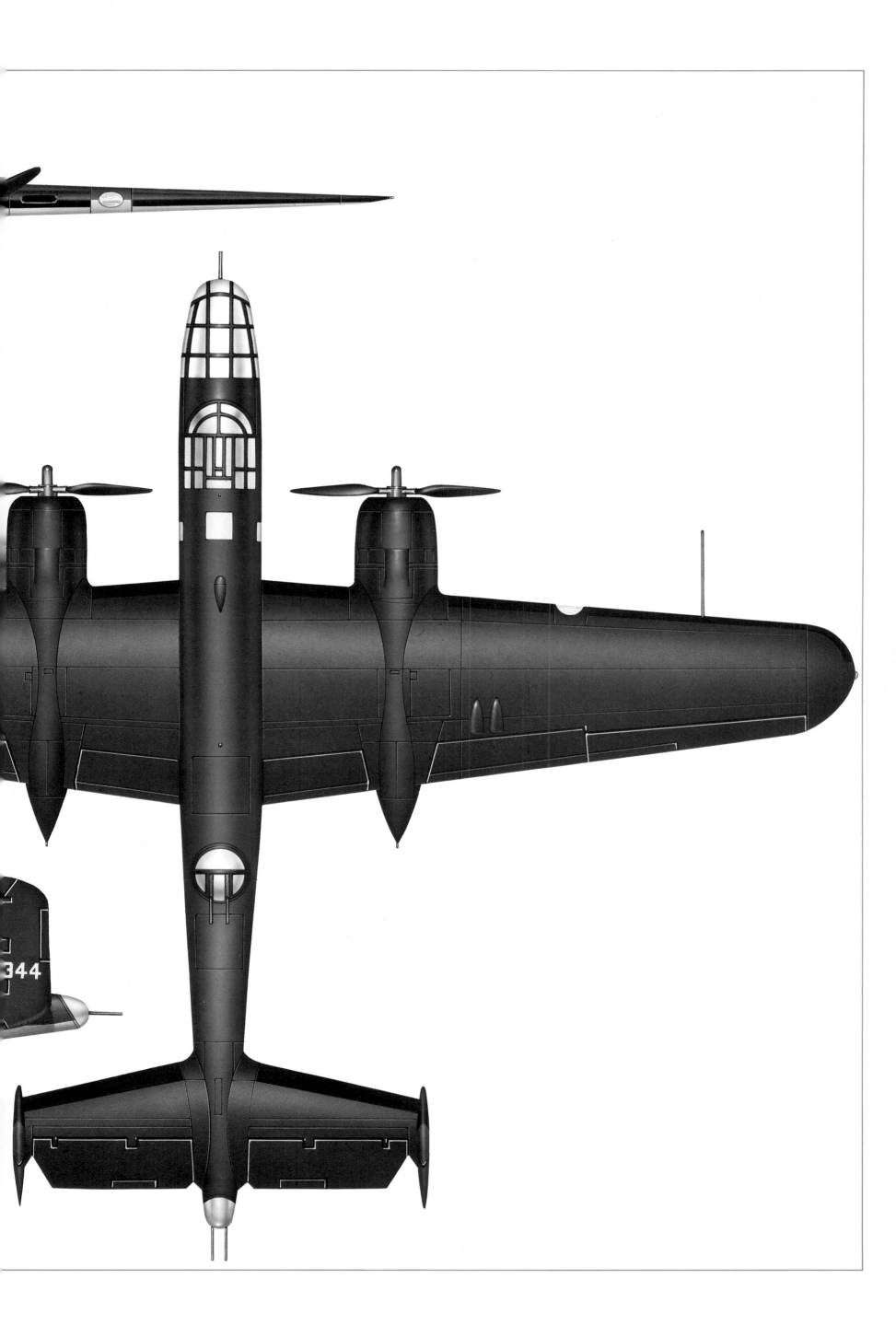

One of the best medium bombers of the entire conflict, the North American B-25 Mitchell was one of the great protagonists of air warfare. More than 11,000 came off the assembly lines in numerous versions between 1940 and 1945, and production was characterized by continuous improvements to the aircraft, as well as an increase in its power, allowing the remarkable features of the original project to be fully exploited. This versatile and efficient two-engine aircraft's intense career lasted well beyond World War II: after having served on all fronts, not only bearing the insignia of the U.S. Army and Navy air forces, but also those of Great Britain, the Commonwealth countries, and the Soviet Union, once the war ended the B-25 was to remain in service until the 1960s, especially in some of the less important air forces.

The original project, designated NA-40, had been launched by the North American company's technicians in 1938 on the basis of specifications issued by the U.S. Army Air Corps requesting a two-engine attack plane and bomber. The prototype made its first flight in January 1939. It was a medium-hight wing monoplane that featured three-wheel forward landing gear and was powered by two Pratt & Whitney R1830-56C3-G radial engines generating 1,115 hp each. These engines were replaced with a pair of 1,369 hp Wright GR-2600-A71 Cyclones, and with this modification the prototype (designated NA-40B) was handed over to the military authorities in March. After only two weeks of flight testing, the aircraft crashed, but there were no longer any doubts concerning its potential: North American was authorized to proceed with the development of the prototype, incorporating a series of modifications into it. The definitive project (NA-62) was completed six months later and immediately went into production (an initial order was placed for 184 aircraft) with the official designation of B-25. The name Mitchell was chosen in memory of General William "Billy" Mitchell, the man who, since 1920, had prophesied the future role of the air force, and whose outspokenness had led to his being court-martialed for insubordination in 1925.

The principal modifications consisted in the widening of the fuselage and the lowering of the wing, from a medium-high to a medium position, in order to improve housing for the crew and the bomb load capacity. The engines were also replaced by two 1,700 hp Wright R-2600 Cyclones. The first B-25 took to the air on August 19, 1940, but showed signs of instability, making further structural modifications necessary. After 24 aircraft had been built, the designation was altered to B-25A, and these 40 aircraft incorporated armor protection for the pilots and fuel tanks. The remaining 120 aircraft ordered in the initial contract were completed as the B version, in which the defensive armament was strengthened through the addition of servo-controlled turrets on the back and in the belly. The production rate then increased with the next two variants, the B-25C and B-25D, delivered at the end of 1941, and of which 1,619 and 2,290 were built respectively. As well as being fitted with a new version of the R-2600 engine, these aircraft were also provided with an autopilot and bomb racks under the wings. The increase in the bomb load also provided the possibility of carrying a torpedo in the case of antishipping attacks. Deliveries to the United States' major allies, Great Britain and the Soviet Union, began with these two versions, and they received a total of 595 and 870 aircraft.

The first operative unit to be equipped with the B-25 was the 17th Bombardment Group, which received the B-25As in the spring of 1941. On April 18, 1942, it was from this unit that the 16 aircraft were chosen to carry out one of the Mitchell's most daring missions: the first air raid on Tokyo. The mission, thought up and commanded by James A. Doolittle, the famous racing pilot of the 1920s, was carried out by B-25Bs that had been specially modified so as to hold the greatest amount of fuel possible. They took off from the aircraft carrier *Hornet*, situated at a distance of 715 miles (1,150 km) from the Japanese coast, and the mission was successfully concluded, although its effects were above all psychological.

color plate

North American B-25B U.S. Army Air Force. Personal aircraft of Lt. Col. James Doolittle with fake machine guns on the tail, during the air raid on Tokyo that took place on April 18, 1942.

Aircraft:	North American B-25C
Nation:	USA
Manufacturer:	North American Aviation Inc.
Type:	Bomber
Year:	1941
Engine:	2 Wright R-2600-13 Cyclone, 14-cylinder radial, air-cooled, 1,724 hp each
Wingspan:	67 ft 9 in (20.60 m)
Length:	53 ft (16.13 m)
Height:	15 ft 10 in (4.82 m)
Takeoff weight:	34,044 lb (15,422 kg)
Maximum speed:	284 mph (457 km/h) at 15,040 ft (4,572 m)
Ceiling:	21,256 ft (6,462 m)
Range:	1,500 miles (2,414 km)
Armament:	5-6 machine guns; 5,207 lb (2,359 kg) of bombs
Crew:	3-6

A formation of B-25 of the 83rd Bomber Squadron in flight over Tunisia in 1943. In order to facilitate identification, a British type "fin flash" has been painted on the tail fin.

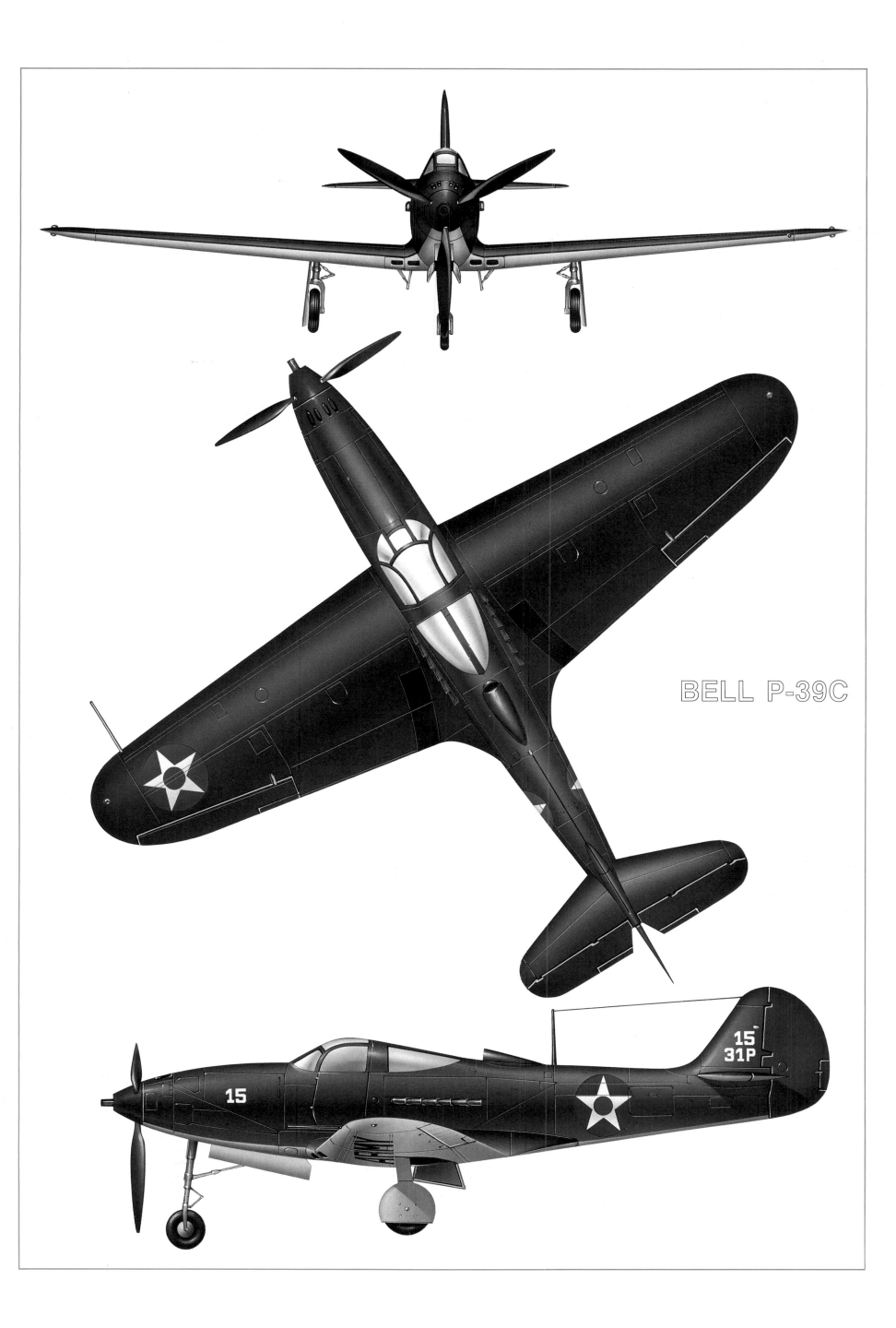

BELL P-39C

Designed as an interceptor, when the Bell P-39 Airacobra appeared it was acclaimed as one of the most advanced combat planes of the time, although ultimately it proved to be rather controversial due to the inadequacy of its engine. This led to it eventually being relegated to the less prestigious role of ground attack. Apart from this, this elegant aircraft still remains one of the most original built by the American aeronautical industry during the war. It was the first fighter in the world to be provided with three-wheel forward landing gear and also the first to have its engine installed centrally (behind the pilot). The latter drove the propeller by means of a transmission shaft that was more than 9 ft (3 m) long and that passed between the pilot's legs.

A total of 9,588 aircraft in several versions was built in all, and almost half of them (4,773) went to the Soviet Union. Despite everything, once the United States entered the war the P-39, together with the Curtiss P-40, was entirely responsible for supporting the front line until its more modern successors, the Lockheed P-38, Republic P-47, and North American P-51, appeared.

In March 1937, Bell presented the project for its revolutionary interceptor to the USAAC. It was literally built around one of the most original and powerful weapons in existence at the time: the American Armament Corporation's 37 mm cannon, which had been tested two years earlier with great success. The design was supervised by Robert Woods, and the result was decidedly original: the aircraft was an all-metal low-wing monoplane in which careful attention had been paid to aerodynamics. The fact that the engine (originally a 1,150 hp Allison V-1710 with supercharger) was installed in a central position was due to the need to install the cannon in the best position, that is to say the nose, together with the two 7.62 mm machine guns. The same need also led to the adoption of the three-wheel forward landing gear, which

had never been used in a single-seater fighter before. However, the central engine, installed in the proximity of the barycenter, also served to improve the aircraft's maneuverability. The prototype, designated XP-39, was ordered in October 1937, and it took to the air for the first time on April 6, 1938. Its performance proved remarkable from the start: without armament and armor, it reached a maximum speed of 390 mph (628 km/h) at 20,050 ft (6,096 m), having taken barely five minutes to reach this altitude. Its characteristics were clearly those of an interceptor, although numerous modifications were imposed on the Bell project by the USAAC authorities. The most important of these included the installation of an Allison engine without a supercharger, and therefore unsuitable at high altitudes. The prototype modified in this way was redesignated XP-39B, and its performance was marked by a notable decline, although it was followed by 12 similar preseries aircraft (YP-39). On October 8, 1939, an order was placed for an initial lot of 80 aircraft in a military version, designated P-39C. Delivery of these aircraft commenced in January 1941.

The next variant, the P-39D, was the first to be produced in any great number and the first to be built for export, although it was also the version that most disappointed the designers. The 675 aircraft ordered by Great Britain were rejected by the RAF after only a few days' service on the English Channel front, in September 1941. The judgment of the pilots was unfavorable: in practice, confronting the German fighters with the P-39 was equal to suicide. Consequently, approximately 200 aircraft were sent to the Soviet Union and a further 250 returned to the United States.

However, the fighter's lack of success did not slow down production. The P-39 continued to come off the assembly lines, not only to satisfy the demands of the U.S. Air Force, but also to satisfy those of the Soviet Union. The final series, the P-39N and P-39Q totaled 2,095 and 4,905 aircraft respectively.

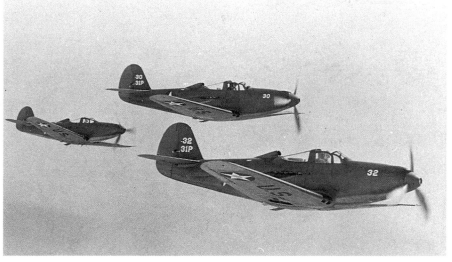

A formation of P-39C used by the 31st Pursuit Group.

A Bell P-39D with attachments for bombs on the belly and enlarged tail fin.

color plate
Bell P-39C 31st Pursuit Group U.S. Army Air Corps - Selfridge Field 1941

An Airacobra P-400 of the version originally built for Great Britain in service with the 67th Fighter Squadron in New Guinea. Note the characteristic shark mouth.

Aircraft:	Bell P-39C
Nation:	USA
Manufacturer:	Bell Aircraft Corp.
Type:	Fighter
Year:	1941
Engine:	Allison V-1710-35, 12-cylinder V, liquid-cooled, 1,150 hp
Wingspan:	34 ft (10.36 m)
Length:	30 ft 2 in (9.19 m)
Height:	11 ft 10 in (3.60 m)
Weight:	7,845 lb (3,520 kg) loaded
Maximum speed:	335 mph (536 km/h) at 13,800 ft (4,200 m)
Ceiling:	29,000 ft (8,900 m)
Range:	600 miles (960 km)
Armament:	1 × 37 mm cannon; 4 machine guns; 500 lb (226 kg) of bombs
Crew:	1

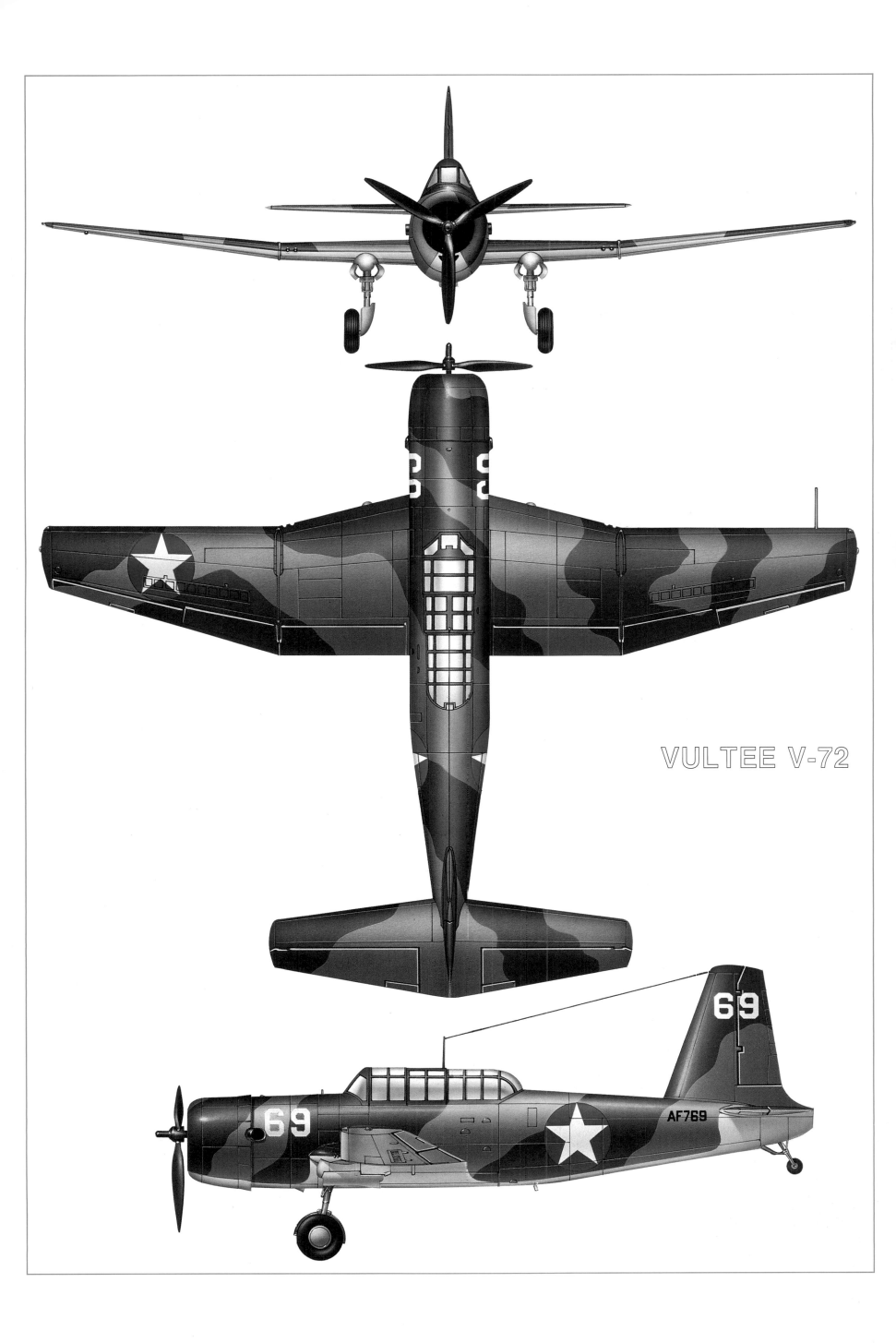

VULTEE V-72

The widespread use of dive-bombers also influenced Great Britain and, in 1940, it explicitly requested the American manufacturer Vultee to create an aircraft of this kind. The result was the Vultee V-72, a large and heavy monoplane that was to assume several designations in the course of its career: A-31 and A-35 in the United States and Vengeance in Great Britain. It never proved to be an exceptional aircraft, and its general inferiority was demonstrated by the fact that even the Royal Air Force (the only one to use it in combat) eventually used it in a theater of war that was less demanding than the European one. In fact, the Vengeance was to remain in service in Burma until the end of the conflict.

The V-72 project was developed by Vultee on the basis of the experience it had acquired during the construction of the V-11 and V-12 bombers, in 1935 and 1939 respectively. The formula chosen was that of an all-metal mid-wing monoplane with retractable landing gear. It was powered by a radial engine, and the two crew members were housed in a long, completely glazed cockpit. The defensive armament consisted of four machine guns on the wings and a mobile position provided with one or two similar weapons for the observer; the aircraft could carry a maximum bomb load of 2,002 lb (907 kg).

In the summer of 1940, an initial order for 700 aircraft was placed by the British Purchasing Commission and was to consist of 400 Vengeance Mk.Is and 300 Mk.IIs. This number was clearly excessive considering Vultee's capabilities and therefore Northrop was also called to participate in the production program. The first prototype took to the air in July 1941, but the need for a series of structural modifications (to the empennage and the aerodynamic brakes) delayed the completion of the aircraft: the first production series Vengeances did not take to the air until June of the following year.

The aircraft of the initial production series, designated A-31 in the United States, were also ordered by the U.S. Army Air Force and subsequently rechristened A-35. Production continued with the appearance of two versions with heavier armament and equipment, and they were designated A-35A and A-35B. A total of 562 of the second variant were assigned to Great Britain (where they were known as Vengeance Mk.IV) and 29 to Brazil. In all, the Royal Air Force received 1,205 aircraft in several versions, out of a total production that, up to September 1944, amounted to 1,528 aircraft.

Once it had been decided not to use the Vengeance in combat in Europe, the career of the Vultee dive-bombers bearing British insignia was generally satisfactory. This decision was made in 1942, when the first aircraft became operational. Experiences in combat had clearly demonstrated that the dive-bombers were extremely vulnerable and that they could carry out their role only if heavily protected by fighters, and even then only against particular targets. In Burma, the Vengeances replaced the two-engine Bristol Blenheims, and they carried out their first mission in July 1943. Later, the RAF ceded some aircraft to Australia and transformed others (Vengeance TT Mk.IV) for use in target-towing.

However, in the United States, the fate of the Vultee bombers was to be less fortunate. They were all used in the secondary role of target-towing and the fact that they were used at all was severely criticized. A high-ranking officer in the U.S. Army described the aircraft as "an evident waste of time, material, and man-power."

---

color plate

Vultee V-72 built for the RAF and requisitioned by the U.S. Army Air Corps, in service at the Gunnery Training Center at Patterson Field in 1941

Aircraft:	Vultee A-35A
Nation:	USA
Manufacturer:	Vultee Aircraft Inc.
Type:	Dive-bomber
Year:	1941
Engine:	Allison V-1710-39, 12-cylinder radial, air-cooled, 1,150 hp
Wingspan:	37 ft 4 in (11.35 m)
Length:	31 ft 2 in (9.49 m)
Height:	10 ft 7 in (3.22 m)
Weight:	8,291 lb (3,756 kg) loaded
Maximum speed:	365 mph (589 km/h) at 15,040 ft (4,572 m)
Ceiling:	29,075 ft (8,839 m)
Range:	950 miles (1,529 km)
Armament:	6 machine guns; 501 lb (227 kg) of bombs
Crew:	2

A U.S. Army Air Corps Vultee A-35.

THE UNITED STATES OF AMERICA

Pearl Harbor, December 7, 1941. After the Japanese attack, damage was as follows: three battleships sunk, a further six damaged to a greater or lesser degree, together with three cruisers, three destroyers, and three minor ships; 188 aircraft destroyed and 159 damaged; 2,403 dead and 1,778 wounded; serious damage to buildings. Barely two hours had sufficed to deal a severe blow to the American military presence in the Pacific and to mark the Empire of the Rising Sun's first victory.

However, Pearl Harbor was not only the beginning of a war that was to continue with increasing violence for three and a half more years, in addition to the one that was already being fought furiously in Europe. It also marked the sudden awakening of the sleeping American giant which, up till then, had not believed that it would become directly involved in the world war. Thus, Pearl Harbor was the beginning of a powerful reaction that was to prove impossible to stop.

On September 1, 1939, the date of the German invasion of Poland, the U.S. Army Air Corps (USAAC) had 2,400 aircraft of all types at its disposal, of which 800 were front-line. A further 2,500 aircraft were in service with the U.S. Navy, and 600 of these were carrier-based. Despite these numbers, it was not a particularly daunting air force: the standard bomber, despite the presence of twenty or so Boeing B-17s, was still the old two-engine Douglas B-18; most of the fighters were Northrop A-17s or Curtiss P-36 Hawks, which were transitional aircraft. In the naval aviation, side by side with the first Northrop BT and Douglas TBD Devastator monoplanes, biplanes such as the Grumman F3F and the Curtiss SBC Helldiver still existed.

The general inadequacy that characterized American military aviation at the time of the outbreak of hostilities in Europe was the result of a series of political, strategic, industrial, and economic factors that had affected its development in the years of peace, leading it along a path that was entirely its own. Apart from delays of an organizational nature, it was above all the industrial network that seemed incapable of achieving its full potential: in 1939, total production of combat planes amounted to 2,195 aircraft, only a few more than the previous year (1,800), and it was not until 1940 that a first noticeable increase in these numbers occurred. In fact, a total of 6,028 aircraft of all types were built, and this increased to 19,445 in 1941. However, production was not stimulated only by domestic requirements, but also and above all by foreign ones in the form of huge requests for military aircraft on the part of France and Great Britain.

Nevertheless, when the United States entered the war, the army air force (which became the U.S. Army Air Force, or USAAF, in June 1941) had 3,305 aircraft ready for service at its disposal, while the navy possessed approximately 3,000. Although these numbers appeared satisfactory on paper, they soon proved to be totally inadequate when faced with the more effective and efficient aircraft used in combat by their direct adversary.

Chronology

1940

May 29. The Vought XF4U-1, prototype of the F4U Corsair, takes to the air. A total of 12,681 were built, and the aircraft was in service from 1943 onward, becoming the most famous American carrier-based fighter of the war.

November 25. The two-engine Martin B-26 Marauder, one of the most widely used American medium bombers of the war, takes to the air. A total of 5,157 were built, and the aircraft went into service in 1941.

December 18. The prototype of the Curtiss XSB2C-1 Helldiver takes to the air. It was destined to replace the Douglas Dauntless as a carrier-based dive-bomber. It did not go into service until the end of 1943, and approximately 7,200 were built.

1941

May 6. The Republic P-47 Thunderbolt, one of the most powerful and effective American fighters of the war, makes its maiden flight. A total of 15,683 were built in numerous versions, and the aircraft went into service during the early months of 1943. After having fought on all fronts, it survived the conflict and served in the air forces of approximately 15 countries.

June. A great impulse is given to the strengthening of the American military aviation with the approval of a program that foresaw the formation of an air force composed of 82 combat units by June 1942, with 7,800 aircraft and 400,000 men.

August 1. The prototype of the carrier-based torpedo plane, the Grumman XTBF-1 Avenger, takes to the air. This aircraft was one of the protagonists of air-sea battles in the Pacific. The Avenger went into service in the spring of 1942, and a total of 9,836 were built. It remained in front-line service until 1954.

BOEING B-17G

297719

Rarely in the history of aviation has an aircraft become both a true symbol of military power and a myth for pilots and crew. This aircraft was the Boeing B-17 Flying Fortress, the first strategic bomber used in combat by the United States during World War II and the aircraft that contributed perhaps more than any other to the annihilation of the Third Reich and the conclusion of the war in Europe. In all, a total of 12,731 B-17s were built (without interruption) in the course of the war, and their most fierce and intensive use is marked by two dates in particular: August 17, 1942, when daylight bombing raids on Europe commenced; and January 27, 1943, when similar bombing raids on Germany began.

Project 299, as Boeing called it, was launched in the summer of 1934, on the basis of specifications issued by the Army requesting a multiengine bomber to be used in the defense of American territory against a hypothetical invader. In particular, the aircraft was to be capable of carrying a bomb load of 2,002 lb (907 kg) for a distance ranging from 1,025 miles (1,650 km) to 2,175 miles (3,500 km) at speeds between 200 mph (320 km/h) and 250 mph (400 km/h). Boeing's designers interpreted the concept of multiengine in its "widest" sense and, instead of concentrating on proposals for an aircraft powered by two engines, following conventional practice at the time, made use of the experience acquired in building the Model 247 civilian transport plane, as well as the solutions studied for a bomber that was still in the process of development, the Model 294. Thus, the prototype assumed the form of a large low-wing four-engine aircraft, with a circular-section fuselage and partially retractable main landing gear. It made its maiden flight on July 28, 1935, and slightly less than a month later, the aircraft revealed its capabilities when it covered a distance of 2,110 miles (3,400 km) nonstop in nine hours. Following official evaluations, the Douglas B-18 emerged as the winner of the contest, although the Boeing project's great potential was also recognized when, on January 17, 1936, an order was placed for 13 preseries aircraft, to be used for flight tests and operational evaluation. The first of these aircraft (designated Y1B-17) took to the air on December 2, 1936, while the others were delivered between March 1 and August 5 the following year.

Following a series of evaluation tests, the results (especially after the installation of Wright engines with superchargers) were so promising that the USAAC requested that it go into production immediately. The first order was placed in 1938, with a request for 39 B-17Bs; in 1939, these were followed by 38 B-17Cs (provided with more powerful engines, armor and better defensive armament), and by 42 B-17Ds, which were basically identical to their predecessors, in 1940. The last two versions were the first to see

combat duty: from May 1941, with the British, and immediately after Pearl Harbor with the Americans. On December 10, 1941, the aircraft that survived the Japanese attack had the honor of carrying out the first American offensive attack of the conflict, against Japanese shipping.

In 1941, a turning point occurred, as far as production was concerned, with the appearance of the B-17E. The entire rear section of the aircraft was radically altered in order to provide greater stability and to allow for the installation of a defensive gun position in the tail. The armament was then increased, with the addition of two turrets, one on the back and the other in the belly, provided with 12.7 mm machine guns. The B-17E was the first to be built in any great number, 512 being produced in all, and it was followed on the assembly lines by 3,400 B-17Fs (the aircraft made its maiden flight on May 20, 1942), with even heavier armament. The total production of the final variant, the B-17G, was much greater and, from 1943 onward, it was sent in increasing numbers to the European front: in all, no fewer than 8,685 aircraft came off the assembly lines. Thanks to experiences in combat, the defensive armament of these Fortresses was increased still further, with the installation of a "chin" turret below the nose.

---

color plate

Boeing B-17G 463rd Bomber Group 15th Air Corps U.S. Army Air Corps - Italy 1945

Aircraft:	Boeing B-17G
Nation:	USA
Manufacturer:	Boeing Aircraft Co.
Type:	Bomber
Year:	1943
Engine:	4 Wright R-1820-97 Cyclone, 9-cylinder radial, air-cooled, 1,200 hp each
Wingspan:	103 ft 9 in (31.62 m)
Length:	74 ft 9 in (22.70 m)
Height:	19 ft 1 in (5.82 m)
Weight:	65,500 lb (29,710 kg) loaded
Maximum speed:	287 mph (462 km/h) at 25,000 ft (7,620 m)
Ceiling:	35,600 ft (10,850 m)
Range:	3,400 miles (5,200 km)
Armament:	13 machine guns; 17,600 lb (7,985 kg) of bombs
Crew:	10

A formation of preseries YB-17s during operative tests in 1937.

A factory fresh B-17G with all metal finish and its formidable defensive armament.

CURTISS P-40C

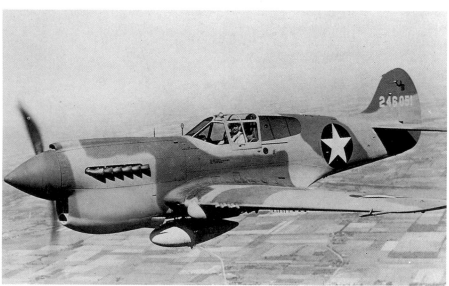

A P-40K with more powerful Allison engine, in flight.

The Curtiss P-40 was not an exceptional aircraft, although paradoxically it was the most important American fighter during the first two years of the war. Its strength, rather than lying in its quality, was to be found in two factors that were fundamental at a time in which all available resources had to be exploited by the Allies in order to fight off attacks in Europe and the Far East: it was immediately available and in a large quantity. In fact, from 1939, no fewer than 13,738 P-40s came off the Curtiss assembly lines, a number that was eventually to place the fighter in third place as far as its total production was concerned, behind rather more effective aircraft such as the Republic P-47 and the North American P-51. Its operational service was also extensive, and it was used on all fronts, in Europe, Africa, the Pacific, and Russia, bearing the insignia of almost all the Allied countries.

The P-40 project was not new at the time it was prepared, in March 1937. In fact, it was based on the airframe of the Curtiss P-36A, and it was planned to replace the original radial engine with an Allison V-1710 12-cylinder liquid-cooled engine. This had been tried out on the tenth P-36A to be built and, modified in this way, the aircraft had taken to the air for the first time on October 14, 1938, with good overall results: carrying a total weight of 6,270 lb (2,840 kg), the aircraft had reached a maximum speed of 340 mph (550 km/h) at 12,230 ft (3,718 m), faster than that of the British Hawker Hurricane, although inferior to the performance of the

Supermarine Spitfire and the German Messerschmitt Bf.109. In 1939, when the USAAC invited bids for the manufacture of a new fighter, the project submitted by Curtiss thus found itself with an overall advantage, due not so much to the inherent potential of the aircraft as to the relative simplicity of launching mass production immediately. On April 27, 1939, the War Department issued an order for the construction of an initial lot of 524 P-40s, although this decision caused a lot of fuss, not so much due to the aircraft being chosen instead of the viable prototypes presented by Bell, Lockheed, and Republic, as to the financial significance of the contract ($12,872,898), the most important of its kind to be approved since 1918.

The first production series P-40 took to the air on April 4, 1940, and almost 200 aircraft had been delivered to the units of the U.S. Air Force by October. At the same time, 140 export models, originally ordered by France, were acquired by Great Britain, where they were known as Tomahawk I and assigned to training duty. The second variant was the P-40B (Tomahawk II in the RAF), which appeared in 1941. It had heavier armament and was provided with armor and self-sealing fuel tanks. This aircraft was the first to see combat duty, bearing British insignia in Africa and American insignia at Pearl Harbor and in China, where it also served in the famous American Volunteer Group, the Flying Tigers.

After a few P-40Bs and P-40Cs had been built, the first important alterations appeared in the P-40D (which made its maiden flight on May 22, 1941, and almost all of the 582 that were built went to the RAF where they were designated Kittyhawk I) and in the subsequent P-40E, delivered in August 1941. These were characterized by different engines and armament, and modified and shortened fuselage and landing gear. The P-40E (2,320 of which were built) was the first to serve in American units based in Europe, in the Mediterranean. Despite the evident limitations of the aircraft, which increasingly proved to be unsuited to the role of interceptor and suited to that of attack, Curtiss continued in its attempts to improve it. In 1942, the P-40F version appeared (1,311 built in all), provided with 1,300 hp Rolls-Royce/Packard Merlin V-1650-1 engines. This was followed in the same year by the P-40K, and by the L, M, and N variants in 1943. In these versions an attempt was made to lighten the airframe in various ways and to increase the power of the engine. The P-40Ns (deliveries began in March 1943) were also the last to serve in the USAAF, and after their production (5,220 aircraft) the assembly lines closed on November 30, 1944.

color plate

Curtiss P-40C 3rd Squadron American Volunteer Group Chinese Nationalist Air Force - Kunming, China 1942

Aircraft:	Curtiss P-40C
Nation:	USA
Manufacturer:	Curtiss-Wright Corp.
Type:	Fighter
Year:	1942
Engine:	Allison V-1710 39,12-cylinder V, liquid-cooled, 1,150 hp
Wingspan:	37 ft 4 in (11.38 m)
Length:	31 ft 2 in (9.50 m)
Height:	11 ft 10 in (3.61 m)
Weight:	9,200 lb (3,900 kg) loaded
Maximum speed:	367 mph (592 km/h) at 12,120 ft (3,685 m)
Ceiling:	29,000 ft (8,840 m)
Range:	850 miles (1,360 km)
Armament:	6 machine guns; 700 lb (317 kg) cf bombs
Crew:	1

A Royal Air Force Kittyhawk in service in North Africa.

FOCKE WULF Fw.190 A-4

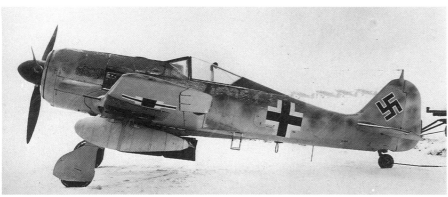

A Focke Wulf Fw.190 A5 with supplementary fuel tanks on the wings and 1,100 lb (500 kg) of bombs beneath the belly.

An Fw.190 A3 in service with the I/SG 1 during takeoff from an airport in occupied France.

An Fw.190 used to launch a Mistel flying bomb.

Considered by many as the best German fighter of World War II, the Focke Wulf Fw.190 was created to flank the already excellent Messerschmitt Bf.109, although it eventually proved to be superior even to its direct rival. Powerful, agile, and versatile, more than 20,000 of this small and compact combat plane were constructed, 13,367 of which were interceptors while the rest were fighter-bombers, from the summer of 1941 up to the end of the war, sharing with the Bf.109 the honor and the burden of constituting the Luftwaffe's front line. From many points of view the careers of the two aircraft were very similar: like the Messerschmitt fighter, the one developed by Focke Wulf was continuously updated and improved in the course of production, exploiting to the full the excellent qualities of the airframe and making the aircraft constantly competitive.

The project was launched in the autumn of 1937, when the German Air Ministry proposed that Focke develop a fighter-interceptor to be produced alongside the Messerschmitt Bf.109. The design team, headed by Kurt Tank, prepared two alternative proposals which differed basically in the type of engine adopted: the first foresaw the use of an in-line Daimler Benz DB 601, while the second was to be fitted with a BMW 139 18-cylinder radial engine, then in the final stages of development. In Germany at that time, designers tended to favor the adoption of liquid-cooled in-line engines for fighters, not only for their great aerodynamic advantages, but above all due to the availability of excellent power plants that had been widely tested and that would probably be developed further in the future. Nevertheless, Kurt Tank managed to convince the ministerial authorities of the effectiveness of the choice of a radial engine for his project. Three principal factors acted in his favor: the fact that the Daimler Benz DB 601 was likely to become less available in the future, as there was already great demand for those produced; the great and promising potential of the new BMW engine; and last but not least, the fact that the radial engine was less vulnerable than the liquid-cooled one, which needed radiators and piping that were easily damaged in combat.

The construction of three initial prototypes was authorized, and the first of these took to the air on June 1, 1939. Despite problems in overheating, the aircraft proved to have excellent flying characteristics and an impressive performance, especially as far as speed was concerned. However, a long time was necessary for the development of the aircraft. It was not until the fifth prototype that the Fw.190 assumed its definitive configuration, following substantial modifications to the fuselage and wings and, above all, the installation of a different engine. In fact, development of the BMW 139 had been abandoned in favor of a 14-cylinder model designated 801. The successful combination of a large radial engine and a slender fuselage, particularly advanced from an aerodynamic point of view, constituted the most striking aspect of the new fighter. Otherwise, the Focke Wulf Fw.190 was an all-metal low-wing monoplane with retractable landing gear, characterized by an almost entirely transparent cockpit that provided the pilot with a remarkable field of vision. The armament initially consisted of four machine guns, two of which were installed in the upper part of the fuselage.

After flight testing, 40 preseries aircraft were ordered, followed by 100 aircraft of the initial variant, the Fw.190 A-1, which went into service in July 1941. In September, the first confrontation with the RAF's Spitfire Mk.Vs took place, and the German fighter proved to be generally superior to the British one, apart from its armament. This was strengthened, together with the engine, in the subsequent A-2 and A-3 series, and updating continued throughout the numerous subseries that followed. Some of the best known were the A-4 of 1942, and the A-5, the A-6, the A-7, and the A-8 of 1943. In these variants, the aircraft was also adapted to the role of fighter-bomber, although this use was explicitly planned for the subsequent versions.

---

color plate

Focke Wulf Fw.190 A-4 personal aircraft of the Commander of the I/JG 54 (1st Group 54 Flight Wing) Luftwaffe - Russian Front 1943-44

Aircraft:	Focke Wulf Fw.190 A-1
Nation:	Germany
Manufacturer:	Focke Wulf Flugzeugbau GmbH
Type:	Fighter
Year:	1941
Engine:	BMW 801C-1, 14-cylinder radial, air-cooled, 1,600 hp
Wingspan:	34 ft 5 1/2 in (10.50 m)
Length:	29 ft (8.84 m)
Height:	12 ft 11 1/2 in (3.94 m)
Weight:	8,770 lb (3,973 kg) loaded
Maximum speed:	389 mph (626 km/h) at 18,045 ft (5,500 m)
Ceiling:	34,775 ft (10,600 m)
Range:	497 miles (800 km)
Armament:	4 machine guns
Crew:	1

GERMANY

The Battle of Britain marked the first turning point in World War II. Apart from the profound effect this event had on the course of the conflict, the summer of 1940 is still remembered as the period in which the first direct confrontation between the two most powerful air forces in the world took place. With the exception of the Great War, never before then had the fate of a nation (in this case, Great Britain) been entrusted entirely to an air force and never before had the aircraft been called upon to play a determining and exclusively strategic role in the success of a military operation.

Aside from being an encounter involving aircraft and men, the confrontation between the Royal Air Force and the Luftwaffe was above all between two entirely different ways of conceiving air warfare. And the loser was, in fact, the way that had, up till then, guided the formation and growth of the German Luftwaffe: doctrines that had been tested in very singular circumstances, such as the Spanish Civil War initially and then the brilliant campaigns carried out in Poland, the Low Countries, and France, had led to a primarily tactical emphasis being given to the aircraft and the structure of the air force of the Third Reich. Faced with the tenacious and fierce reaction of the British, which differed greatly from previous experiences, the practical results of those bloody weeks of continuous attacks against Great Britain revealed the Luftwaffe's lack of effective strategic strength. The effects of this followed one after another in a chain reaction: although the Heinkel He.111 and Dornier Do.17 medium bombers, considered the best in the world, were fast, they proved to have an inadequate range and to lack effective defense against the attacks of the British fighters. Consequently, the formations had to be continually protected before, during, and after missions, and, hampered in this way, the other-wise excellent Messerschmitt Bf.109s were unable to carry out their optimum role as interceptors, penalized above all by their range. The performance of the aircraft most publicized by Goering, such as the Junkers Ju.87 *Stuka* and the Messerschmitt Bf.110 *Zerstörer*, did not prove to be any better, and they were painfully vulnerable when faced with the Supermarine Spitfires and Hawker Hurricanes.

Thus the myth of the Luftwaffe's invincibility did not last beyond the first year of the war, although the first defeat, with the annulling of Operation Sea Lion, which was to have concluded with the invasion of Great Britain, did not detract from the immense potential of the German air force. A year later, Hitler launched Operation Barbarossa against the Soviet Union, turning his back on the age-old adversary and searching for new ones and, inexorably, German military involvement became enormous, on fronts all over the world. During this phase and throughout that of Germany's final defense, the Luftwaffe was to remain feared and powerful, nourished unceasingly by an industrial production that was at an extremely high qualitative but above all quantitative level. In September 1939, when the invasion of Poland took place, out of an air force that had 4,840 of the most modern and competitive front-line aircraft at its disposal, including 1,750 bombers and 1,200 fighters, the German aeronautical industry had already established a monthly production rate of 1,000 planes. In 1939 alone, no fewer than 8,300 aircraft of all types were completed. The following year, this figure rose to 10,800 and, in 1941, to 11,800 in an almost frenetic "crescendo" that was to continue at a rate that was equal to the violence of the conflict, despite the destruction and devastation that the Allied bombers caused to the entire German production network.

Chronology

1940

Summer. The first Focke Wulf Fw.200 C-1 *Condors* become operative in the 1st and 3rd Groups based at Bordeaux-Mérignac and at Trondheim-Vaernes. This large four engine aircraft originated in 1936 as a civilian transport plane and found its optimum role in long-range naval reconnaissance. Unfortunately known as the "Scourge of the Atlantic," the *Condor* remained in service until 1943, before being relegated to transport duties.

1941

May 20. The Luftwaffe organizes an impressive air raid, known as Operation Merkur, in order to conquer Crete. Approximately 650 aircraft were drawn up for battle and destined to provide cover from the air for the paratroops, as well as 80 or so gliders and almost 700 three-engine Junkers Ju.52s to carry the paratroopers and for glider-towing. The operation was a success, although at a high price in terms of men and aircraft.

September 14. The giant Messerschmitt Me.321 attack gliders are used for the first time in action, during a mission carried out on the island of Saaremaa in the Baltic. However, these aircraft proved to be difficult to tow and were replaced by the Me.323, fitted with four engines capable of keeping the aircraft in flight at altitude after a towed takeoff.

October 2. The third prototype of the Messerschmitt Me.163 rocket-engine interceptor piloted by Heini Dittmar reaches 623 mph (1,004 km/h) in horizontal flight. This aircraft, the only one of its kind and the first ever to be powered by a rocket-engine, went into service on May 13, 1944, and just under 300 were built. Christened *Komet*, the Me.163 was used against the huge formations of Allied bombers.

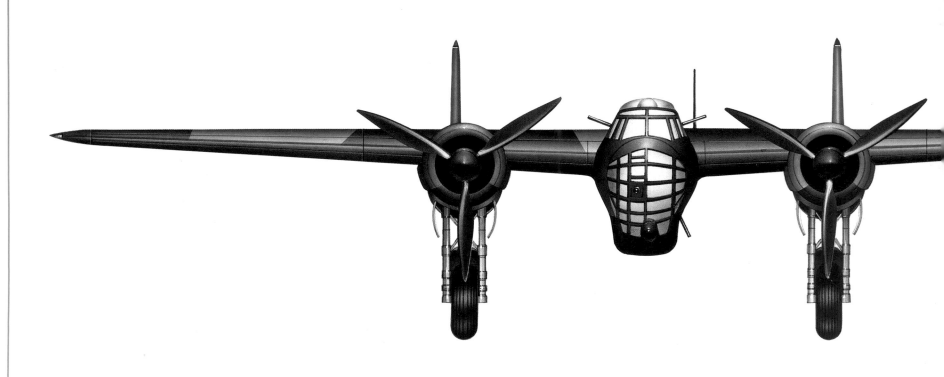

DORNIER Do.217 E-2

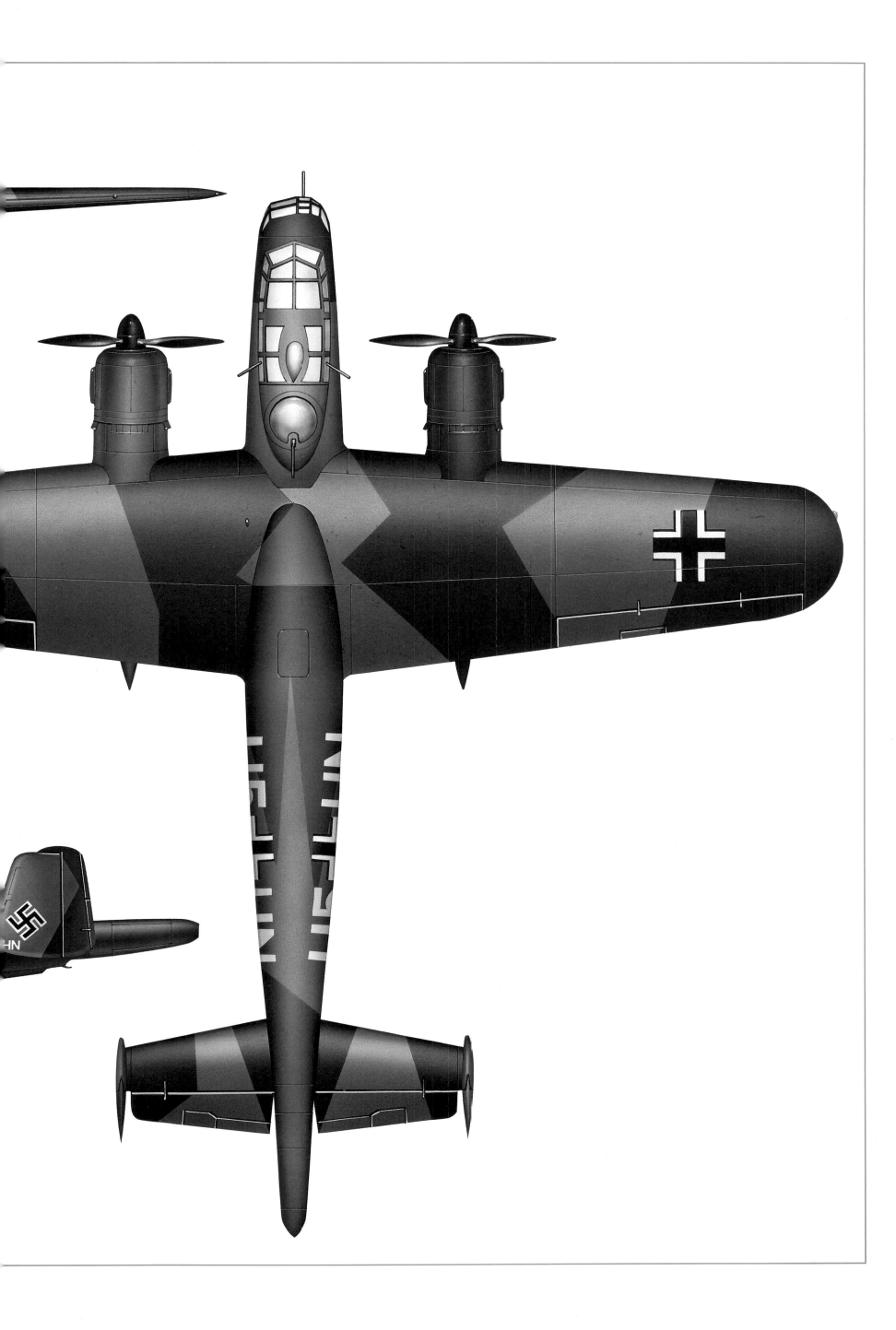

The family of two-engine Dorniers, which originated with the Do.17 in the early 1930s, holds a place in the history of aviation as one of the Luftwaffe's best known and most widely used aircraft. This series of combat planes was developed continuously in numerous versions and derivatives and remained in production for the duration of the conflict, operating on practically all fronts and in a great variety of roles. The success of the original Do.17 model led Dornier to develop a larger and more powerful version of the aircraft. This was the Do.217, an aircraft that embodied the potential of the original project to the full and that was to make its mark due to its great versatility. The approximately 1,900 aircraft built in various versions from 1940 until June 1944 were in fact used with great success as bombers, reconnaissance planes, torpedo planes, and night fighters.

The project went ahead while production of the Do.17 was in full swing, and the prototype took to the air for the first time in August 1938. Although its overall layout was the same as that of its predecessor (it resembled the Do.17s of the final production series in particular), the aircraft was characterized by a longer and wider fuselage that terminated beyond the empennage in an ''umbrella-type'' aerodynamic brake (with four sections that opened up, braking and stabilizing the aircraft during dive-bombing, although this solution did not prove to be very effective, and this method was eventually eliminated). It was powered initially by a pair of Daimler Benz DB 601 A engines, generating 1,075 hp each.

During flight testing of the first prototype a series of problems emerged, especially as far as the aircraft's stability was concerned, and it crashed after barely a month of trials. Preparation of the other prototypes went ahead, with special study being dedicated to the installation of the various types of engine foreseen in the project, but proved to be long and laborious. In fact, the definitive configuration was reached only in the Do.217 V9 prototype, during the first weeks of 1940. The main change was represented by a notable deepening of the entire fuselage, necessary to rationalize and increase to the maximum the installation of the bomb load, the fuel tanks, and other equipment. In addition, in place of the two in-line Daimler Benz engines, powerful BMW 801 series radial engines, capable of generating more than 1,500 hp at takeoff, were installed.

The first production series, the Do.217 A reconnaissance plane (of which only eight were built), was derived from this prototype and went into service in 1940. The principal variant, the Do.217 E, appeared in the same year and went into service as a bomber in the spring of 1941. In the aircraft of the initial E-1 series, the defensive armament consisted of a small 15 mm MG 151 cannon and five 7.9 mm MG 15 machine guns, all of which were installed in the front part of the aircraft, and a 4,415 lb (2,000 kg) bomb load inside the fuselage. This was followed by the E-2 and E-3 series, in which the defensive armament was modified, with the addition of a turret on the back provided with a 13 mm machine gun. Among the numerous versions that followed were the Do.217 E-2/A-4 torpedo plane; the Do.217 E-2/A10, used for naval patrol and able to carry 4,415 lb (2,000 kg) of bombs under its wings; and the Do.217 E-5, capable of launching two Hs.293 type radio-guided bombs.

The development of the bomber versions proceeded alongside that of the night fighter variants. Toward the middle of 1942, the Do.217 K appeared, characterized by a redesigned nose and more powerful armament: eight machine guns for defense and a maximum of 8,830 lb (4,000 kg) of bombs, including two radio-guided ones (Do.217 K-2). The Do.217 M series was prepared in the same year, marking a return to the use of in-line engines, with two 1,650 hp Daimler Benz DB 603s. In all, a total of 1,541 aircraft were built in the bomber version, and 364 in the night fighter version.

color plate

Dornier Do.217 E-2 5th Staffel 2nd Kampfgeschwader (5th Squadron 2nd Bomber Group) Luftwaffe - France 1941

Aircraft:	Dornier Do.217 E-1
Nation:	Germany
Manufacturer:	Dornier Werke GmbH
Type:	Bomber
Year:	1940
Engine:	2 BMW 801 MA, 14-cylinder radial, air-cooled, 1,580 hp each
Wingspan:	62 ft 4 in (19.00 m)
Length:	59 ft 8 1/2 in (18.19 m)
Height:	16 ft 6 in (5.03 m)
Weight:	33,070 lb (14,980 kg) loaded
Maximum speed:	320 mph (515 km/h) at 17,060 ft (5,200 m)
Ceiling:	24,600 ft (7,500 m)
Range:	1,430 miles (2,300 km)
Armament:	1 × 15 mm cannon; 5 machine guns; 4,415 lb (2,000 kg) of bombs
Crew:	4

A Dornier Do.217 bomber with its under surfaces blacked out for use at night.

MACCHI M.C.202

A Macchi M.C.202 in service with the 91st Squadron bearing the insignia of the rearing horse.

A Macchi M.C.202 is started manually at an airport in Libya.

color plate

Macchi M.C.202 personal aircraft of the Commander of the 153rd Gruppo Caccia 53rd Stormo (153rd Fighter Group 53rd Flight Wing) *Regia Aeronautica* - Libya 1942

Aircraft:	Macchi M.C.202
Nation:	Italy
Manufacturer:	Aeronautica Macchi S.p.A.
Type:	Fighter
Year:	1941
Engine:	Daimler Benz DB 601A-1, 12-cylinder V, liquid-cooled, 1,175 hp
Wingspan:	34 ft 8 1/2 in (10.58 m)
Length:	29 ft 1 in (8.85 m)
Height:	9 ft 11 1/2 in (3.02 m)
Weight:	6,480 lb (2,937 kg) loaded
Maximum speed:	372 mph (600 km/h) at 18,050 ft (5,500 m)
Ceiling:	37,700 ft (11,500 m)
Range:	475 miles (765 km)
Armament:	2 machine guns
Crew:	1

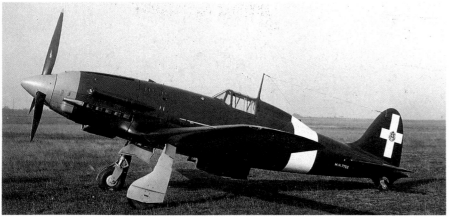

A factory fresh Macchi M.C.202 bearing national insignia and without operational markings.

Following the M.C.200 *Saetta* (Arrow), the family of combat planes presented by Macchi during the second half of the 1930s was enriched by a new, more effective model in 1940. This was the M.C.202 *Folgore* (Thunderbolt), an aircraft that is generally remembered as the best Italian fighter to go into service with the *Regia Aeronautica* during World War II, due to its characteristics, the number that were built, and the extent to which it was used. The *Folgore* went into service in November 1941 and was operational on practically all fronts. From May 1941 to August 1943, more than 1,100 aircraft came off the assembly lines, production being divided between Macchi itself, Breda, and SAI Ambrosini.

The factor that allowed the effective airframe of the model 202 to be exploited to the full was the availability of the German Daimler Benz DB 601 engine and, from this point of view, the construction of the new Macchi fighter marked a fundamental turning point in the design philosophy that the Italian aeronautical industry had followed up till then. This foresaw the adoption of radial engines, whose development had been preferred over that of liquid-cooled in-line engines. This was in spite of the excellent results achieved in the latter sector during the various aeronautical contests held in the period between the two world wars, and in the Schneider Cup in particular.

However, the limitations of this choice had been apparent right from the earliest combat experiences: the fighters of the so-called first generation (Fiat G.50 and Macchi M.C.200) had proved to be totally inadequate and uncompetitive, not only as far as their immediate adversaries, the British, were concerned but also compared to the products of Germany, Italy's principal ally. The most obvious disadvantages derived not only from the clear aerodynamic limitations imposed by the installation of a massive radial engine, but also, and above all, from the relatively limited amount of power available. Thus, in the search for an effective in-line engine which was indispensable to keep up with the evolution of the most advanced combat planes, Italy turned to Germany for help, first through the importation of the Daimler Benz DB 601s, and second, through Fiat and Alfa Romeo building them on license. This choice, albeit delayed, proved to be the right one: in fact the various variants of the Daimler Benz engines made the creation of the *Regia Aeronautica*'s most prestigious fighters possible, that is to say, the excellent Macchi M.C.205, the Fiat G.55 and the Reggiane Re.2005s belonging to the "5 series," all of which, despite their late arrival and the fact that only few were built, soon figured among the best of the entire conflict. They also placed the Italian aeronautical industry on a competitive level with other nations.

In 1940, on its own initiative, Macchi acquired a German engine and began studies for a new version of the *Saetta*. Its designer was Mario Castaldi, and the prototype, which made its maiden flight on August 10, retained the wings and empennage of its direct predecessor. On the other hand, its fuselage was entirely different and was characterized by carefully studied aerodynamic lines and a closed cockpit. As soon as flight testing began, the performance of the new aircraft proved to be clearly superior: its maximum horizontal speed touched 372 mph (600 km/h), while in ascent it could reach 19,735 ft (6,000 m) in five minutes 55 seconds. Its only defect lay in its armament, which was limited to two 12.7 mm machine guns synchronized to fire through the propeller. However, attempts were made to improve this in the later production series, adding another two weapons of smaller caliber under the wings.

A large number of *Folgore* were ordered immediately, and the aircraft made its operational debut in Libya, although it was soon to be used on all fronts in Africa, as well as the Balkan and Russian fronts and in the Mediterranean. It continued to be used after the armistice, both in the units of the cobelligerent air force and those of the *Repubblica Sociale Italiana*. The surviving aircraft were used for training by the *Aeronautica Militare Italiana* until 1948.

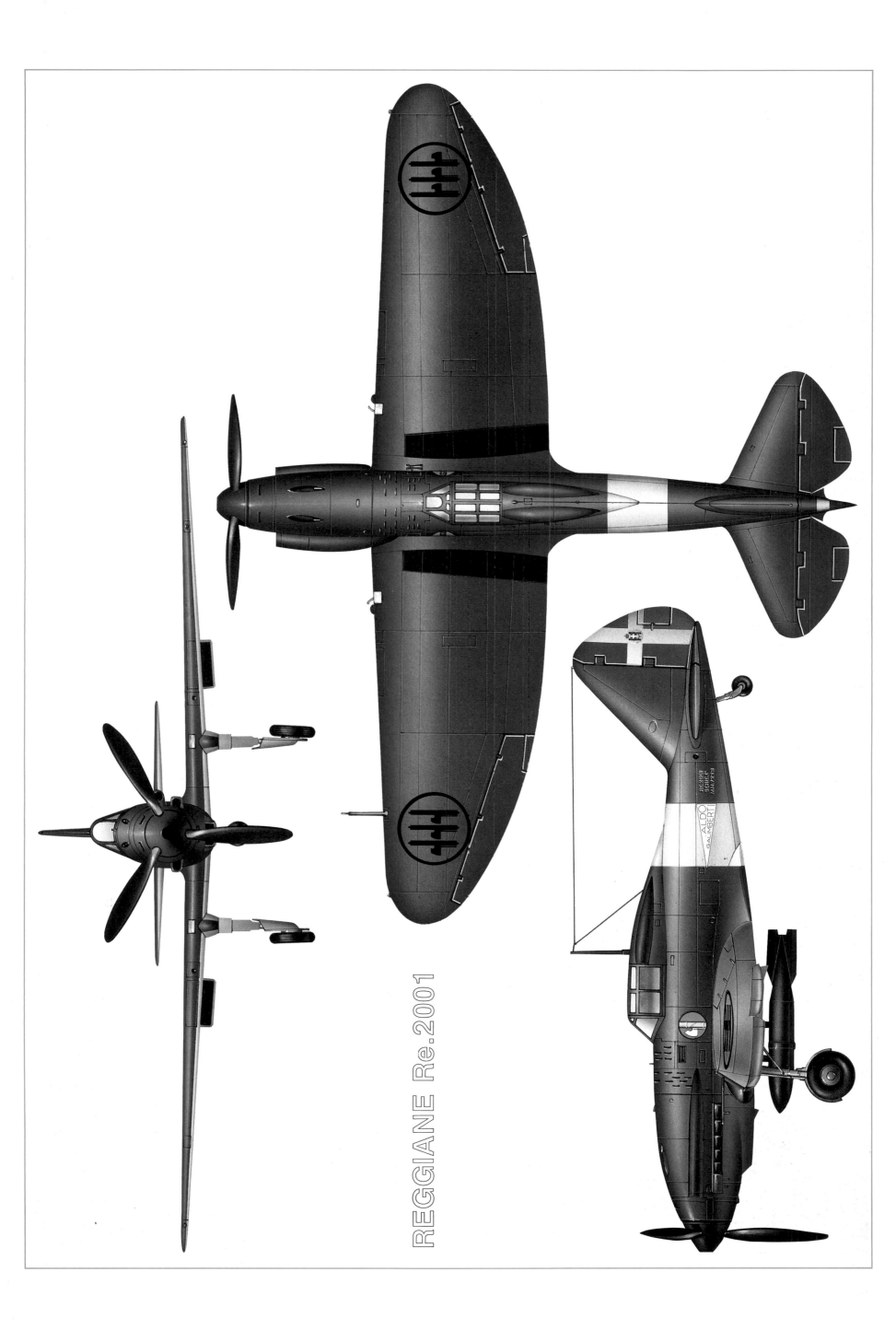

REGGIANE Re.2001

The most famous and widely used of the first generation Italian fighters during the war were the Fiat G.50 and the Macchi M.C.200. However, in addition to these two aircraft, a third contemporary combat plane deserves to be remembered, not so much for its extremely limited operative career in the *Regia Aeronautica*, as for the excellent qualities of its design, which were truly innovative for the time. This aircraft was the Reggiane Re.2000, designed by Roberto Longhi and Antonio Alessio in 1938. Paradoxically, the aircraft was rejected by the authorities and was produced for export, serving brilliantly bearing the insignia of Hungary and Sweden.

The Re.2000's lack of success led the Reggiane company to develop a new version of its fighter, which was designated Re.2001. The determining factor behind this decision was the availability of German Daimler Benz DB 601 engines. Longhi and Alessio had adapted these to the airframe of the original project, in place of the Piaggio P.XI radial engine. The result, which appeared as a prototype in June 1940, was a notably improved aircraft with a good overall performance. However, this was to be as unlucky as its predecessor had been. In fact, delays in completing the aircraft (in order to carry out a long series of modifications requested by the *Regia Aeronautica*) and a relative shortage of engines (priority was given to the Macchi M.C.202 fighter as far as these were concerned) limited the Re.2001's operative career. Only 237 aircraft were built, and they were never used in the role of interceptor, but relegated to the role of fighter-bomber initially, and then to that of night fighter.

The initial delays meant that the first production series aircraft were not delivered until June 1941, almost a year after the prototype's maiden flight. In fact, Reggiane's technicians were forced to substantially redesign the wing in order to adapt the structure and conformation of the internal fuel tanks to the requests of the authorities. Production also went ahead slowly: approximately 40 aircraft were completed in 1941, a further 100 or so in 1942, and the rest in the first half of 1943. As well as the original fighter version, there were two variants: the CB (fighter-bomber) and the CN (night fighter), both with more powerful armament. The first could carry a 220 lb (100 kg) or 550 lb (250 kg) bomb externally. In exceptional circumstances it could also carry a 1,412 lb (640 kg) bomb. In the second variant, the machine guns on the wings were replaced by the two 20 mm cannons housed in external nacelles.

The Re.2001 started its operational career at the beginning of December 1941, and it was assigned to three *Squadriglias* of the 2nd Fighter Group of the 6th *Stormo*, being used mainly in the Mediterranean and in Italy itself as a night fighter. Following the armistice, several of the surviving aircraft served in the cobelligerent air force and, to a lesser extent, in that of the *Repubblica Sociale Italiana*. Five aircraft served for several years in the *Aeronautica Militare Italiana* after the war had ended.

Mention should be made of several prototypes that Reggiane developed from the Re.2001 in an attempt to improve the original project still further. The first of these was the Re.2001 *bis*, on which modifications, mainly of an aerodynamic nature, were carried out. It began flight testing in April 1941, piloted by Francesco Agello, who held the world speed record for seaplanes. Its performance proved to be excellent, and it reached speeds of over 38 mph (60 km/h) faster than the original version of the aircraft. The second prototype was the Re.2001 *Delta*, in which an attempt was made to overcome the problems caused by the shortage of available Daimler Benz engines by installing the 840 hp Isotta-Fraschini Delta V-12 air-cooled engine as an alternative. The fighter, successfully tested toward the end of 1942, crashed in January of the following year and an order for 100 aircraft was cancelled.

---

color plate

Reggiane Re.2001 22nd C.T. Group *Regia Aeronautica*. One of the two aircraft that attacked the aircraft carrier H.M.S. *Victorious* in the Mediterranean on August 12, 1942, hitting it with 1,412 lb (640 kg) bombs that failed to explode.

Aircraft:	Reggiane Re.2001
Nation:	Italy
Manufacturer:	Officine Meccaniche Reggiane SpA (Caproni)
Type:	Fighter
Year:	1941
Engine:	Daimler Benz DB 601 A-1, 12-cylinder V, liquid cooled, 1,175 hp
Wingspan:	36 ft 1 in (11.00 m)
Length:	27 ft 5 in (8.36 m)
Height:	10 ft 4 in (3.15 m)
Weight:	6,700 lb (3,040 kg) loaded
Maximum speed:	349 mph (563 km/h) at 17,700 ft (5,400 m)
Ceiling:	36,000 ft (11,000 m)
Range:	684 miles (1,100 km)
Armament:	4 machine guns
Crew:	1

One of the two Reggiane Re.2001s that attacked H.M.S. *Victorious* in the Mediterranean on August 12, 1942.

ITALY

Hampered by programs based on outdated criteria and by a general lack of planning and foresight on the part of its high command, the *Regia Aeronautica* faced the first year of the war in conditions that definitely could not be compared with those of its German ally. On June 10, 1940, the day on which Italy declared war, the potential of its military aviation was as follows: 3,296 aircraft at its disposal, in Italy itself, in the Aegean area, and in Libya. Of these, 1,796 were front line: 783 bombers, 594 fighters, 268 observation planes, and 151 reconnaissance planes. Despite this number, the most worrying fact consisted in the quality of the aircraft, especially the fighters, which were generally inferior to those of the enemy. Almost half of the *Regia Aeronautica*'s fighters were Fiat C.R.42 biplanes, while the rest consisted of the more modern but still inadequate Fiat G.50 and Macchi M.C.200 monoplanes. Moreover, effective attack aircraft did not exist, while the bombers were perhaps slightly better, consisting of Fiat B.R.20s and SIAI Marchetti SM.79s.

The first year of the war only emphasized this situation. The unfortunate experience of the Italian Air Corps in Belgium, from October 1940 to January 1941, was significant, and it represented the *Regia Aeronautica*'s one and only appearance in the most fierce and advanced theater of war at the time, that of the English Channel. In the course of almost two months of fighting, the best aircraft available, such as the C.R.42 and G.50 fighters and the B.R.20 bomber, revealed their limitations, proving to be outdated, vulnerable and inadequate.

An attempt to remedy this situation was made once the war had begun, especially in the fighter sector. This recovery was made possible thanks to the help of Italy's German allies. At that time, the most serious problem hampering the design of a combat plane that could compete with those produced by Great Britain and Germany was the lack of an effective in-line engine. As it was impossible to develop an extremely powerful and reliable engine of this type in time, it was decided to import the excellent Daimler Benz DB 601 from Germany in order to equip a second generation of fighters.

This engine, with its remarkable characteristics, its lengthy operative career, and its great potential for development, proved to be the ideal choice, and it made it possible for the Italian aeronautical industry to make the necessary qualitative leap. Several versions of the Daimler Benz engine eventually equipped all the second — and third — generation Italian fighters. The first exponents were the Macchi M.C.202 *Folgore* (Thunderbolt — considered the best overall of the entire conflict) and the Reggiane Re.2001. Both of these aircraft went into service in 1941, the second year of the war.

Although there was a remarkable improvement at a qualitative level, progress at a quantitative level was rather less effective, as the aeronautical industry was hampered by a shortage of raw materials. In 1940, aeronautical production amounted to 3,257 aircraft, and the following year this figure increased only slightly, with a total of 3,503 being built.

Chronology

1940

June. The prototype of the Reggiane Re.2001 fighter makes its maiden flight. It was the first of a new generation of interceptors powered by German Daimler Benz DB 601 engines, built on license by Alfa Romeo. Due to a laborious preparation phase, the fighter did not go into service until December 1941.

June 5. The prototype of the SIAI Marchetti SM.84, a three-engine bomber destined to replace the SM.79, makes its maiden flight. A total of 309 were built, although the bomber never equaled its predecessor. It went into service in February 1941.

June 28. Death of Marshal Italo Balbo, governor of Libya and protagonist of the "golden years" of the *Regia Aeronautica*. His aircraft was shot down by mistake near Tobruk by Italian antiaircraft fire.

August 10. The prototype of the Macchi M.C.202 *Folgore* fighter takes to the air. It was the *Regia Aeronautica*'s first truly competitive combat plane and one of the best Italian fighters overall of the entire conflict. It went into service in May 1941, and more than 1,100 were built.

August 28. The Campini Caproni CC2 makes its maiden flight. In this aircraft, jet propulsion, albeit in a hybrid form, was experimented, thanks to a radial engine that drove a supercharger that, in its turn, sent compressed air to an afterburner. The aircraft was not followed up.

1941

May. The 274th Squadriglia Bombardamento a Grande Raggio (Long Range Bomber Squadron) is formed, the first and only unit to be equipped with the four-engine Piaggio P.108.

September. The *Regia Aeronautica* orders the first 200 Reggiane Re.2002 *Ariete*, the best fighter-bomber to go into service in the Italian air force. Although it was delivered beginning in March 1942, this aircraft did not go into service until July 1943, when it was too late.

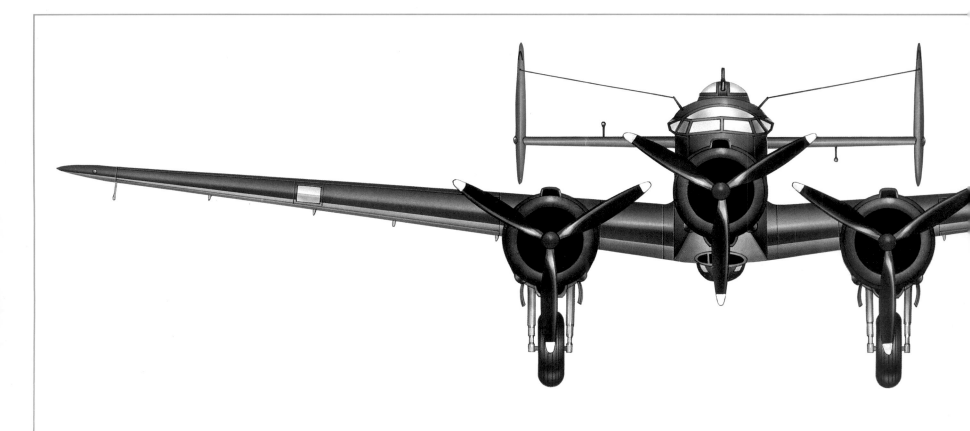

SIAI MARCHETTI SM.84 bis

8-2

In 1940, the three-engine formula, typical of Italian aeronautical production during the war, was enriched by the addition of a new bomber, the SIAI Marchetti SM.84. This aircraft was designed to replace the SM.79 *Sparviero* (Sparrowhawk), but it never succeeded in equalling its more illustrious predecessor. This was principally due to its lack of maneuverability, making it anything but ideal in the role of torpedo-bomber, and to the general lack of reliability of the Piaggio P.XI engines.

The project was launched by Alessandro Marchetti in 1939, and the prototype made its maiden flight on June 5 of the following year. Marchetti based his proposal for the aircraft on the airframe of the SM.79, retaining the same wings and substantially modifying the fuselage and empennage. The former, with its more advanced and innovative lines, lacked the characteristic hump on its back, while the latter was doubled. As far as the rest of the aircraft was concerned, it was characterized by its low wings, airframe of wood and steel tubing, and it had a covering of fabric, plywood and duraluminum. The aircraft was powered by three Piaggio P.XI radial engines, generating 1,000 hp each and driving three-bladed variable-pitch metal propellers. The defensive armament consisted of four 12.7 mm machine guns, installed in a turret on the aircraft's back and in three defensive positions, two on the sides of the fuselage and the third in the belly. The bomb load could be housed either under the wings or inside the belly. In the first instance, four rockets or two torpedos or bombs weighing up to 3,532 lb (1,600 kg) could be carried, while in the fuselage the maximum bomb load was 2,207 lb (1,000 kg).

performance had led to the realization of a *bis* version, with modifications mainly to the wing (now provided with a positive dihedral) and the cockpit, as well as to the ventilation of the engine and the torpedo-launching controls. However, these aircraft also went into service with bomber units, where they were to be operative until the armistice. In July 1943, the 43rd *Stormo* was the only unit to be equipped with the SM.84, and by September 8, it had 30 of these aircraft at its disposal. A further 130 bombers, of which only a hundred or so were effective, were distributed among several of the *Regia Aeronautica*'s supply centers.

Following the armistice, a certain number of SM.84s were requisitioned by the Germans which incorporated a dozen or so aircraft into the 132nd Transport Group, where they served until the end of the war.

Original model of the SIAI Marchetti SM.84 with horizontal wing.

An S.M.84 *bis* with positive dihedral wing in original factory finish before assignation to its unit.

Prior to the prototype's maiden flight, several tests had been carried out with a specially modified SM.79, provided with double empennage and 860 hp Alfa Romeo engines, and the aircraft's performance and potential had proved to be generally satisfactory. This was not so when the prototype of the SM.84 began its evaluation tests: it immediately proved to have a series of problems, especially during takeoff and landing, principally caused by the great weight of the wings and by the inadequacy of the vertical empennage. Moreover, the Piaggio engines proved to be unreliable and difficult to build.

Despite these problems, a large number of the new bombers were immediately ordered by the *Regia Aeronautica*, with an initial request for 246 aircraft placed almost at the same time that the prototype appeared and evaluation tests began. Eventually, orders were to amount to 309 aircraft.

The SM.84 began its operational career with the 41st Bomber Group in February 1941, and several months later it was also to serve with the 36th *Stormo Aerosiluranti* (Torpedo Flight Wing). The three-engine aircraft served in the role of torpedo plane for almost a year, until the autumn of 1942, when it was reassigned to bomber units. In the meantime, attempts to improve the SM.84's

color plate

SIAI Marchetti SM.84 bis 8ª Squadriglia 25° Gruppo Bombardamento 7° Stormo (8th Squadron 25th Group 7th Flight Wing) *Regia Aeronautica* - Sicily (Italy) 1942

Aircraft:	SIAI Marchetti SM.84
Nation:	Italy
Manufacturer:	SIAI Marchetti
Type:	Bomber
Year:	1941
Engine:	3 Piaggio P.XI RC40, 14-cylinder radial, air-cooled, 1,000 hp each
Wingspan:	69 ft 7 in (21.20 m)
Length:	58 ft 10 in (17.93 m)
Height:	15 ft 1 in (4.59 m)
Weight:	29,330 lb (13,288 kg) loaded
Maximum speed:	268 mph (432 km/h) at 15,000 ft (4,600 m)
Ceiling:	25,900 ft (7,900 m)
Range:	1,137 miles (1,830 km)
Armament:	4 machine guns; 3,532 lb (1,600 kg) of bombs
Crew:	5

CONTENTS